Events of Yesteryear

W9-ASK-507

1900

THE TURN OF THE CENTURY

Noël Bosetti
English translation by Christopher Sharp
Picture research by Martine Mairal

Silver Burdett Press
Morristown, New Jersey

A World of a Billion and a Half Inhabitants

In the early morning fog of May 9, 1900, the whistle of the steamship *SS Ionia* began to blow. Two weeks had passed since the boat's departure from Piraeus. During that period, it had made a stopover in Naples before passing the Strait of Gibraltar and heading west for New York. On board was the most precious cargo imaginable — hope. Hope was in the hearts of the 450 passengers who had left such places as Russia, Austria-Hungary, and Italy, fleeing poverty and in search of a better life.

They were leaving a Europe whose population had doubled within a century, exceeding 400 million inhabitants. The continent was the home of scientists, inventors, industrialists, workers — all of them authors of the Industrial Revolution. These people had made more progress in one hundred years than their forefathers had made since the Stone Age.

The death rate was declining. The horrible famines that had decimated the countryside were no more than a memory. Boats and trains could now rapidly and safely transport abundant and relatively low-cost food. Advances in the field of medicine made it possible to cure illnesses that up until then had been fatal. Since the time Louis Pasteur demonstrated the existence of disease-causing bacteria in 1880, good hygiene had become common and the number of infections diminished. With a longer life span, Europe's population grew, though its people did not have more children than in the previous century. Workers and employees living in cramped city dwellings thought twice before having large families.

The immigrants' first destination at the end of their long voyage was Ellis Island. There they had to undergo a medical examination and give their name, date, and place of birth in a language U.S. immigration officials often did not understand. Once the last formality was accomplished, the door opened to the promised land. With an American first name and a last name whose spelling was arbitrarily decided by the all-powerful man behind the register, they could now begin a new life in the home of the Statue of Liberty whose torch lit the port of New York.

Big cities attracted a steady flow of migrants from the countryside. They came in search of work. Forty-five million Europeans lived in one hundred and thirty five cities that had populations of more than one hundred thousand.

Life was difficult in Europe at the turn of the century, despite the progress that had been made. A decline in wheat prices ruined the small farmer. Unemployment benefits were not available for workers and their homeless families. From Norway to Sicily and from Ireland to the Ukraine, nearly one million emigrants left their homelands in 1900. Anonymous and courageous participants in one of the largest migrations in world history, they headed for countries like South Africa and its gold mines, Brazil, where huge fortunes were being made in coffee and rubber, and for Australia, New Zealand, Canada, and Argentina. But it was the United States that attracted the greatest number. The large open spaces of the New World, the spirit of the pioneers in the Far West, gold diggers, and cattle ranchers were all dreams of the poorest of Europeans. The American millionaire, the self-made man, was in their eyes living proof that anything was possible if one really wanted to succeed. The standard of living in the rest of the world was far below that of prosperous Europe. India and, to a greater extent, China had frightening death rates. Famines, wars, and floods all took their toll of victims who numbered in the hundreds of thousands and sometimes even millions. In Africa, 120 million people lived huddled alongside rivers or in a few coastal towns. They had a very high infant mortality rate. In Cameroon, over two-thirds of the newborn babies died before reaching the age of one! Life expectancy did not exceed twenty-one years of age! Never had there been greater inequality in the living conditions of people.

The world's population in 1800 and 1900
(in millions of inhabitants)

	1800	1900
Europe	187	401
Asia	602	937
Africa	90	120
North America	6	81
Central and South America	19	63
Australia and Oceania	2	6
Total	**906**	**1608**

European emigration in 1900...

Italians	240,000
British	180,000
Hungarians	130,000
Russians	100,000
Others	150,000

...and some countries of destination

United States	450,000
Canada	80,000
Argentina	60,000
Brazil	40,000
Australia	45,000

Birth and death rate in 1900
(per 1,000 inhabitants)

	B	D
Great Britain	30	18
Germany	36	23
France	22	21
Russia	49	34
United States	30	17

The illustrated supplement from the September 19, 1909, edition of the French newspaper Le Petit Journal *relates in a caricature the race to reach the North Pole.*

Peary and an Eskimo from his expedition pose in front of their ships protected inside a Greenland fjord.

The Last of the Great Explorations

Wearing a colonial hat, dressed in white, and overseeing a cohort of porters, the explorer was the hero of an adventure nearing its end during the latter part of the nineteenth century. For the past four hundred years, European navigators and explorers had discovered unknown continents and islands, sailed up the large rivers in America, penetrated the mysteries of Asia's jungles and Africa's forests and savannas, and crossed burning deserts and the frozen wastes of Siberia. Livingstone, Stanley, Brazza, just to mention a few, gave their names to places on the map whose blank areas of unexplored territories gradually disappeared.

What was there left to discover in 1900? Robert E. Peary, an American engineer, said to himself, "The only man still capable of equaling the glory of Christopher Columbus is the one who will stand at the North Pole with 360 degrees of longitude beneath his feet." That man was to be himself! Already, in 1895, the Norwegian Nansen thought he would be able to reach the Pole by letting his ice-imprisoned boat drift with the ice floe. When he realized he was going to miss his target, he left the boat with his friend Jonhansen and their 28 dogs and headed directly north. Lost in the frozen emptiness, they were miraculously saved by an English expedition.
In 1896 the Swede

Andrée flew off in his balloon for the Pole. His remains and those of his companions were found in 1930!

Peary attributed these failures to a lack of preparation. For nearly twenty years, he learned to live in the cold. Twice he crossed Greenland in order to become accustomed to the climate. Accompanied by a team made up mainly of Eskimos, he decided to tackle the 435-mile ice floe separating Greenland from the North Pole. Twice he failed. His frostbitten toes had to be amputated, but nothing could stop him. His courage and tenacity appealed to the American people, who were enthralled with his project. A fund-raising campaign enabled him to build a powerful ship capable of cutting through the ice floes. He christened the vessel in honor of Theodore Roosevelt, then President of the United States.

On August 23, 1908, the *Theodore Roosevelt*, arrived at Cape Sheridan, west of northern Greenland, to winter in. On February 22, 1902, 19 sleds, each pulled by seven dogs, started off over the frozen expanse. Fighting the cold and trying to avoid leads, large channels of water that abruptly separate the ice, the expedition reached 87 degrees North latitude. From there Peary launched his final assault with a party of five — four Eskimos, Ootah, Egingwah, Seegloo, and Ooqueah; and Matthew A. Henson, a black man who had been on the explorer's earlier expeditions. On April 7, Peary planted the American flag and took possession of the Pole on behalf of the United States. For the souvenir picture, Henson had the honor of holding the flag.

All that was left to conquer was the South Pole. This resulted in one of the most dramatic races in the history of exploration. Competing were the Norwegian Roald Amundsen and the Englishman Robert Scott. Amundsen had already participated in Arctic expeditions and dreamed of equaling Peary's feat of reaching the North Pole. As for Robert Scott, he had already spent time in Antarctica. On June 15, 1910, he left England with his team. After a long stopover in New Zealand, he arrived on the frozen continent and built a base. While setting up food depots along the future route, he received news that Amundsen had already left. The race began.

Amundsen's plan was simple. The main part of the expedition had to reach the last food depot. From there, only four men carrying the bare essentials would continue on to the goal. Each would have his own sled. As for the dogs, they would be fed the meat of their less resistant companions who would be killed by the men along the way.

Scott met with a series of misfortunes. His tractors broke down as soon as the group left. The ponies, which he preferred to dogs, were incapable of climbing the steep slopes of the 10,000-foot-high mountains. They had to be killed one after the other. Pulling the sleds themselves, Scott and his four companions drew nearer to the South Pole. The tracks they encountered in the snow confirmed what they had been fearing all along. Amundsen was ahead of them. On January 18, 1912, they reached a small tent over which flew the Norwegian flag. Inside, there was some food and a letter of congratulations signed by Amundsen. The five men were dismayed!

The journey back was pure agony. Exhausted, they were forced to walk 370 miles to reach their camp. Food was bitterly lacking and therefore severely rationed. The first to die from exhaustion was Evans. He had gone crazy and passed away on February 17. One month later, Oates, whose feet and hands were frostbitten, left the tent and walked toward death so that his three companions would not be held back. The sacrifice was useless, for Wilson, Bowers, and Scott died snowbound in their tent, just 10 miles away from the food depot that could have saved their lives.

A French party wades through a creek in the African savanna. A black soldier proudly carries the French tricolor. This is one of the countless prints in the magazine Le Tour du monde *that popularized the colonial idea among the French people.*

Giants of the Sea

In 1900 the unprecedented fight to rule the seas, which had begun in the first half of the nineteenth century between the world's last great sailing ships and modern steamers, was entering its last round. Clippers were gigantic ships with steel hulls that could have four, five, or even six masts. Slender and long and sometimes measuring more than 325 feet by 49 feet with a razor sharp bow, they could reach from 13 to 18 knots (15 to 21 mph) in a favorable wind. Thirty days, however, were needed to cross the Atlantic and nearly three months to sail from Australia to England. On the deck, or balancing on the yards more than 160 feet above the sea, crews of about two hundred men raised and pulled on sails and worked to the rhythm of the leading seaman's shrill whistle.

Built in European and American shipyards until 1910, clippers continued to sail to China and Australia at the beginning of the century. Still profitable on these long voyages, they transported tea and wool. Some ended their career by supplying the boilers of their competitors with coal. High speed was not the reason for the steamship's victory. Its regularity was. Whether it traveled through storms or over a placid sea, the steamer was never late in an era when time meant money.

Very practical for short distances, small steamers, or "tramps," as they were sometimes called, transported wheat, iron ore, or coal, depending on what was needed. The first large specialized ships also began to appear. Oil tankers carried Russian or American oil to Europe. Refrigerated ships supplied England and Germany with fresh meat from Argentina or the United States.

In 1900, however, oceanliners ruled the sea. The major sailing companies were Germany's Hamburg-Amerika and England's Cunard and White Star. They waged a merciless battle to win the blue ribbon for crossing the Atlantic in record time. Between 1900 and 1914, more advanced techniques made it possible to build ever larger and more rapid steamships. Dry docks nearly 1,000 feet long were needed to make such colossal works. Two or three boats of the same kind were generally built in the shipyard. Several thousand workers participated in the task, using enormous quantities of steel. Some propellers reached 20 tons, and the assembly of a hull required from 2 to 3 million bolts, which alone weighed more than 1,000 tons! These giants were propelled by no less than twenty to thirty boilers supplying steam engines, and often by a turbine. In 1900 the largest oceanliner, Hamburg-Amerika's *Deutschland*, measured 590 feet long, had a tonnage of 16,500, and did 15 knots (17 mph). In 1914 the *Bismarck*, from the same company, measured 918 feet, weighed 56,000 tons, and did 27 knots (31 mph). It could cross the ocean in less than five days!

These giants of the sea could carry up to 2,500 passengers with a crew of nearly 1,000 members. They were truly floating cities, with a church, restaurants, coffee shops, tennis courts, and a swimming pool. All levels of society were represented. The poor traveled in third-class dormitories on the lower deck, with the heat and continuous noise of the machines. For them, the 300 francs paid for the journey between the French port of Le Havre and New York represented several years of savings.

On the upper promenade deck, millionaires, elegant women, and ambassadors, as well as adventurers and swindlers, who found an ideal "place of work," were never without something to do. Activities on

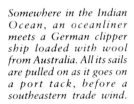

Somewhere in the Indian Ocean, an oceanliner meets a German clipper ship loaded with wool from Australia. All its sails are pulled on as it goes on a port tack, before a southeastern trade wind.

The tragedy of the Titanic
Measuring 882.5 feet long, 125 feet wide, and 190 feet high from the keel to the top of its smoke-stacks, the Titantic *was a floating palace and the pride of the White Star Company. On April 10, 1912, it left the English port of Southampton. On board were 2,207 passengers and crew thrilled to participate in the inaugural voyage of the world's most beautiful ship. Declared "unsinkable" at the time of inspection, the Titantic only had 20 lifeboats with spaces for 1,178 persons! On Sunday, April 14, at 11:35 P.M., passengers still in the smoking room where the orchestra was playing ragtime tunes suddenly felt a jolt. A cracking sound could be heard. The Titanic had just hit one of the numerous icebergs the radio had been reporting since early afternoon. The opening gash was enormous. It was more than 300 feet wide on the starboard side of the hull. Captain Smith ordered the ship to be evacuated. At 12:45 A.M., the first lifeboat was lowered into the water. The radio operator launched history's first S.O.S. (Save Our Souls). The* Titanic *was tipping increasingly forward and dangerously dipping its prow. The orchestra was now playing hymns, which the passengers in turn began to sing. At 2:15 A.M., a big wave swept across the gangway. The ship stood up straight, perpendicular to the water, and threw hundreds of persons into the freezing water. They tried to hold on to floating debris. At 2:20 A.M. the ship disappeared into the ocean depths. At 4:10 A.M., the captain of the oceanliner the* Carpathia *took the first survivors on board. All together they would number only 705!*

board ranged from theater shows and roulette at the casino to sumptuous dinners with more than twenty courses. First-class passengers paid huge sums to have a sitting-room-cabin with fashionable furniture and a private bath. A steward, whose white uniform was as richly decorated as that of the captain, was on hand to provide every comfort.

In the cities the rickshaw was the main means of conveyance for colonists in Indochina and Europeans living in trading posts in China. For the natives, it became a hated symbol of colonial exploitation.

Dividing up the World

"People are suffocating on the old continent." Speaking before the Chamber of Deputies in Paris in 1882, Léon Gambetta justified colonization. Twenty years later, England, France, Germany, Belgium, Italy, and the Netherlands had conquered Africa, southern Asia, and Oceania, while czarist Russia was expanding in Siberia. More than 600 million people were living in colonial empires governed by European powers.

Curiosity, the thirst for knowledge, and a taste for the exotic compelled explorers to go out in search of new territories. But the countries of Europe, backed by governments and large trading companies, had more powerful interests. The Continent's young industries needed copper, rubber, timber, coffee, and cocoa to manufacture various products. What better place to obtain all this than in tropical countries? Furthermore, in order to sell their own products, new markets had to be created.

Still another reason for colonial expansion was ideological. Many Europeans reasoned that the benefits of technical progress should not be confined to Europe, especially when steamships and railroads made formerly faraway places so near. The West would soon be able to export its wealth and civilization, disseminate the "highlights" of its culture, and offer the "consolation" of its religions! These ideas were upheld by traders, geographers, missionaries, and politicians. Such ideas inspired journalists to write impassioned articles aimed at gaining the support of their readers when critics opposed the colonizing nations. In this race to divide the world and obtain as big a piece as possible, England and France were in the lead.

Present in the Indies since the eighteenth century, sea-ruling Britain intended to dominate the shipping line between London and Calcutta. In 1882 Britain took over Egypt and thus obtained control of the Suez Canal, built in 1869 by the Frenchman Ferdinand de Lesseps. Great Britain conquered Sudan in 1898, after twenty years of war against the ferocious resistance of the local Muslim populations.

The French made forays inland from their trading posts on the western coast of Africa. Their aim was twofold. They were out to explore and at the same time conquer the areas they discovered. Soldiers were recruited from among the subjected peoples for the colonial army, which served as the driving force behind these expeditions. Commanded by a corps of young, courageous, and ambitious officers, the army relied on hardened noncommissioned officers who trained and supervised the young recruits. Every year during the dry season, its columns set off to fight the troops of local kings and chiefs if they did not accept "France's protection." Those who resisted were often massacred. After a bloody two-year war in Asia, France imposed the 1885 Treaty of Tientsin on China, making Indochina a French possession. Thirteen years later, considering the island of Madagascar an important stopover on the route to Asia, France annexed it and set up a military governor responsible for keeping order.

When their paths crossed, the colonial powers were more often opposed to one another than in agreement. The Russians and English vied with each other to control

Afghanistan, while the English and French competed for the possession of numerous regions in Africa.

But Germany, a latecomer to colonization, was the main contender in a race from which it was excluded. It managed to create two colonies in East and South West Africa and occupied Cameroon and Togo. Morocco, which was one of the few African countries to have remained independent in 1900, was of particular interest to Germany. In 1905 the German Emperor William II arrived in Tangier. "I recognize the sultan of Morocco as a free sovereign," he declared. But France attempted to impose its authority over the country. In 1911, after a crisis that brought France and Germany to the verge of war, Germany agreed to France's taking over Morocco…provided it (Germany) received a piece of the Congo.

It was a strange period in time when territories and their inhabitants were the subject of bargaining, when meridians and parallels determined both frontiers, the language in which the natives were educated, and the color of the flag they saluted and for which some were to die during the war of 1914–1918!

At the foot of the citadel of Fez, Morocco, General Gouraud's entire staff posed for a picture. In the background can be seen a detachment of spahis, the pride of the French colonial cavalry.

In 1899, the English poet Rudyard Kipling paid tribute to White colonizers:

Take up the White Man's burden —
Send forth the best ye breed,
Go bind your sons to exile
To serve your captives' needs;
To wait in heavy harness
On fluttered folk and wild —
Your new-caught, sullen peoples,
Half-devil and half-child.

Take up the White Man's burden —
No tawdry rule of kings,
But toil of serf and sweeper —
The tale of common things

Performed on every stage in Europe since its creation in Paris in 1865, *L'Africaine,* an opera by G. Meyerbeer, was set during the period when Vasco da Gama discovered the sea route to India. In the great aria of Act IV, the hero sings of the fascination Europeans had for the tropical world.

"Beautiful country, sweet garden,
 Behold the glittering temple,
 Oh paradise come forth from the water
 Blue sky, pure sky
 Before my gleaming eyes,
 You are mine! Oh new world
 My country
 The bright red land is ours,
 This Paradise regained is ours!
 Oh wonderful treasures, behold the marvels,
 New World, you are mine."

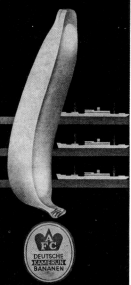

DEUTSCHE KAMERUN BANANEN

This advertisement for a German banana company in Cameroon shows that colonization also meant exotic fruit on European tables.

Africa in Colonial Times

Djambala, colony in the French Congo, January 1, 1900.

Dear Papa and Mama,

It's 85°F out and raining. Yesterday I celebrated the new century. What a strange New Year's party. I spent three hours in my hut talking to Sergeant Bouchard and drinking absinthe, which my servant, Béké, kept on serving us. We talked about all sorts of matters and especially about the home country. He is from the Pas-de-Calais. For him, the Colonial Army was a way of avoiding the mines. He began as a corporal in the Tonkin army and was in Lang Son in 1885. He's the one who taught me what little I know about Africa since I came to relieve Lieutenant Faure six months ago. The real Africa I see now has nothing to do with the Africa I imagined when graduating from Saint-Cyr [a famous French military academy]. Although I still occasionally pursue rebels who ravage one of the villages I must protect, I spend most of my time overseeing this part of the savanna, two hundred kilometers north of Brazzaville. I'm an important person here and my role is mainly that of a judge. I'm responsible for deciding on a number of small conflicts which at first sight may seem petty but which can degenerate into wars between clans if I do not bring some order to the situation. I'm faced with the task of continually convening tribal chiefs, listening to everyone, saying little, and reaching a decision of the kind the chiefs themselves would have arrived at. It is the only way of winning over their confidence. I really need it, because it's not with my 50 men that I'm going to be able to put down a rebellion. Every morning, my day begins with the raising of the flag. Bouchard makes sure that all his men are up in seconds flat and treats them roughly. His brutality goes beyond what is tolerated in the instruction manual, but he's managed to make soldiers out of them. It's a pleasure to see those strong and sturdy blacks during maneuvers. They sing "The Republic calls to us…We shall conquer or we shall die…" When the time comes, I'm sure they'll be brave and heroic. On the other side of the village square, the White Fathers have built our church. There are two of them, one from the Ardennes and the other from Brittany. One is as cold as the other is stocky, but they're both saints! Up before everyone else, Father Pierre goes into the bush country to teach the Bible in distant villages, while Father Tanguy works in the clinic caring for infected wounds and those bedridden with fever. Their medical chest only contains iodine and a few grams of precious quinine. These two priests are so well known that many natives put their superstitions aside and convert to our religion (this doesn't, however, prevent them from consulting their witch doctors). Prayers are the first French words small black children learn. We need a school teacher to educate the brightest. Some of them are far from stupid. I always have two or three tagging along who salute me with the order "attention!" as soon as they see me. I have tried to teach them to read with an alphabet I brought along. Their progresss is amazing! But what good are our efforts when there are the powerful companies? In order to exploit the forests and plant cacao trees, they use thousands of natives handed over to them by unscrupulous chiefs. The great Brazza, our governor, was sent back to Paris two years ago for having defended the poor blacks. What good was it to have fought the slave trade in Sudan if this outrageous situation is tolerated? I read in the Echo de Paris, which I receive three months late, that French officers dishonored our army. Lieutenants Voulet and Chanoine were on their way to Chad from Niger at the head of a column of 250 men and pillaged the villages along their way, massacring the inhabitants. As if this was not bad enough, they killed Colonel Klobb, who had come to arrest them. The tragedy took place on July 14th.

Reports in Le Petit Journal keep me abreast of events in South Africa. The Boers are giving the English a rough time. They will be forced to swallow some of their pride. It wouldn't bother me in the least …but you probably know more about this than I do, lucky Parisians! I'm going to leave you now and look forward to soon being among you. (The colonel has hinted that my request for a leave this summer should be granted.)

Your son Pierre.

From 1899 to 1902, South Africa was a battleground. The British fought to obtain control of the rich mining region of Transvaal from the Boers, colonialists of Dutch origin who had been living there for the past thirty years. Poorly armed but instilled with a fierce desire to win, the Boers inflicted heavy losses on the English armies. The English were victorious, however, and annexed Transvaal.

In 1898 Major Marchand, pictured here in official talks with the emperor of Ethiopia, Menelik, was entrusted with the mission of penetrating Sudan and reaching the Nile. When arriving in Fachoda, his column encountered the English army of Lord Kitchener. Too small in number to resist, the French soldiers retreated. France and England were on the verge of war!

15

China — from Empire to Republic

On June 22, 1912, six months after the Republic was proclaimed, this young Chinese visited the Forbidden City in Peking, the "Saint of saints" of the Celestial Empire.

Since the time he was born in 1882 in a village in Shandong, 310 miles south of Peking, Liang Zhu-deng had only known poverty and hardship. He was only five years old when the dikes of the great yellow muddy river, the Hwang Ho, broke, flooding the province and causing the death of more than a million people. Since then, the dikes had not been repaired. The mandarin and local officials kept the little money provided by the governor for the

necessary work. They organized a work party to fill in the largest holes. In return for gifts, rich peasants were exempt from having to participate. As there was not enough farmland to provide food for the entire family, Liang left for Tientsin. This was in the terrible year of 1895, when the Japanese, after a lightning war, destroyed the Chinese fleet and imposed a humiliating treaty on the empire. After this war, foreigners, or "pink-skinned dogs," as the Chinese called them, descended on the country like vultures.

The foreigners took advantage of the weakness of the emperor Kuang-hsü, manipulated by the old and fearsome empress Tz'u Hsi, to impose their "protection." They built railroads and exploited and controlled the territories they crossed. France took the south, England the center, Russia the north, and Germany and Japan divided up the rest. They set up military bases and maintained war fleets. The Americans were the only ones not to take anything but, like the others, they hoped to benefit from the Chinese market and make large profits.

Liang found a job working in a soap factory in Tientsin. He had to work twelve hours a day, six days a week, and was often beaten by the foreman. For his efforts, he received in all a few copper sapecs (small coins) and a bowl of noodles. Some of his comrades at work belonged to the secret organization of the "fists of justice." They swore they would throw the foreigners out of China. They criticized the government of arrogant mandarins who bowed before the barbarians and accepted the presence of Christian missionaries who had come to preach their religion against the ancestors' traditional form of worship. Liang joined the secret organization and trained in sacred boxing. His head covered with a red turban and his waist decorated with a large scarlet belt, Liang participated in deadly raids. The "Boxers," as they were called by the foreigners, ransacked the homes of Chinese Christians.

In Peking the empress Tz'u Hsi decided to favor the Boxers' action. On June 13, 1900, they entered the city from the south. The empress gave the 1,000 foreigners residing in Peking one week to leave the capital. But the Boxers were impatient to get rid of them and killed the German minister Ketteler. Panic-stricken, the foreigners found refuge in the neighborhood where the foreign legations were located. On June 21, Tz'u Hsi ordered a siege to be laid against them. It was to last 55 days. With his companions, Liang attempted to overrun the walls from which 500 soldiers steadily fired back. But the Boxers did not have modern guns or rifles. In Europe the various governments were for once able to reach an agreement and decided to send a rescue army. "Show no mercy and take no prisoners!" the emperor of Germany William II said to his soldiers as they left for China.

On August 14 a combined force of 16,000 Japanese, English, Germans, Russians, Austrians, Italians, Americans, and French entered Peking. They rescued the legations where 76 adults and 6 children had been killed. Revenge turned into a slaughter and thousands of Chinese were massacred without a trial. The imperial palace was ransacked. Its treasures were plunder worthy of ancient wars. The empress, who had been forced to flee Peking, had to agree to pay an enormous compensation.

Liang managed to escape to his home province by avoiding the main roads, which were patrolled by soldiers. His beautiful dream of independence had been shattered. But like many Chinese, he no longer thought the emperor and empress were worthy of ruling in the name of heaven and the gods. As a sign of revolt, he cut off his braid of hair. For more than 250 years, the Chinese had been forced by the Manchu emperors to wear the infamous braid.

Rebellion was in the air everywhere. The imperial armies were having an increasingly hard time restoring order. On October 10, 1911, an uprising occurred in Wuchang, a large city in central China, and spread within a month to the rest of the country. The foreign powers did not intervene, preferring to reach an agreement with those at the head of the revolt.

On January 1, 1912, a republic was proclaimed, putting an end to an empire that had lasted more than two thousand years. However, the change of regime did not affect the foreigners who, more than ever before, remained the true rulers of the country.

Tz'u Hsi, the fearsome dowager empress, is pictured here near the end of her life. A member of the emperor's court at an early age, she became his favorite and managed to reign in place of his children from 1875 to 1908. Opposed to all reform, living secluded in the Summer Palace, she was the mastermind behind all plots. Realizing that she was about to die, she is suspected of having had the successor to the throne executed on the eve of her death!

17

British India

E mpress of India since 1857, in 1900 Queen Victoria reigned over the largest colony on the planet. India was the jewel and pride of the British Empire as well as the heart of its economy. From the mountains in Kashmir to the jungle in Ceylon, from the deserts in Rajasthan to the Ganges delta, 300 million Indians lived under the sovereignty of the viceroy in Delhi.

Beginning with trading posts along the coast of India in the eighteenth century, the English gradually took control of the internal provinces. The powerful East India Company had its own soldiers and for a long time waged wars in the name of the British crown. After signing protectorate treaties with local sovereigns, the company shipped tea, spices, cotton, and jute to England. When the East India Company was abolished in 1858, the English government took over its activities, which became purely administrative. Because the British in India numbered fewer than 140,000 in 1900, the English relied on Indian princes to keep order. British officers recruited a native army made up mainly of Sikhs, a people united by a religion and traditions of their own.

In order to rapidly transport farm produce to ports, the English built the finest network of railroads in colonial times. The cities of Bombay, Madras, and especially Calcutta grew in size and exceeded one million inhabitants. The Indian population, however, paid the price of colonial occupation. In the countryside, most peasants owned little land. They had to rent plots from owners who forced them to grow cotton rather than rice or wheat. The fees imposed represented up to 80 percent of the crop! In certain regions, peasants died from hunger while their fields yielded excellent harvests of indigo, a plant used in dying cotton fabric! Only the Punjab, in the northwestern part of the Indian peninsula, experienced increased wheat growing thanks to dams built by English engineers.

The industry of cotton fabrics supplied work for numerous villages. However, Eng-

The splendors and riches of India can be seen in this picture. The maharajah of Kapurthala has invited the sovereigns of the Punjab to a reception.

lish and even Indian traders imported low-priced cotton fabrics "made in England," which ran local producers out of business. Nevertheless, Indian capitalists managed to set up a young industry. Two hundred textile factories were operating in 1900.

The English did not do anything to change the system of castes that governed Indian society. Under this system, one's social status was determined by the caste of one's birth. In India there were four chief castes: Brahmans (priests), Kshatriyas (the military), Vaisyas (merchants and farmers), Sudras (laborers). The lowest social group, the "untouchables," as they were called, were outside the caste system. They received the most degrading and poorest-paying jobs.

But the British could not oversee their immense empire without the help of the Indians. In the countryside, owners collected taxes for them. Several provinces remained directly under the authority of more than 700 local princes called maharajahs. They were often linked to the English, and their sumptuous life-style was in total contrast with the extreme poverty of their subjects.

In the cities, English schools educated the sons of the Indian upper middle class to become civil servants or employees in the railroad companies. The richest Indians sent their children to England to study in boarding schools and universities around London.

It is with these English-speaking Indians exposed to Western culture that the first

ideas of independence were born. In 1885 the Congress party was created. In the beginning, its members timidly demanded the right to autonomy. In 1906 they became more assertive. Anti-English riots broke out and were brutally quelled by the army. A campaign to boycott English goods encouraged Indians to wear only clothes made in India. In 1908 a lawyer of Indian origin residing in South Africa, where he was defending the rights of his compatriots living under a pitiless racist regime, published a book entitled *Indian Autonomy*. His name was Ghandi, and he became the father of independence.

A family of English colonialists surrounded by servants added a touch of exoticism to Victorian austerity.

Japan During the Meiji Era

Japan, the only independent power in Asia, went from the Middle Ages to the Industrial Revolution in thirty years. For two centuries, the Japanese refused Western influence, closing their ports to European ships. The country was ruled by 276 powerful lords who overburdened the peasants with taxes and imposed order through the intervention of their warriors, the samurais. Lords and samurais obeyed a strict code of honor based on the respect of ancestors and the practice of martial arts. They despised labor and considered money to be evil and vulgar.

In 1867 Mutsuhito became emperor and proclaimed his reign the Meiji. He was only fourteen years old, but he had no intention of being deprived of the power exercised in reality by the shogun, the most important lord in the country. In 1868 he supported a group of young samurais in overthrowing the shogun and left his palace in Kyoto to take up residence in the palace of his adversary in Tokyo. The city was declared the capital of the country. This Meiji revolution was to transform Japan into a modern State. In order to avoid suffering the same fate as China, which had been completely taken over by the Western powers, the Japanese realized that they had to create an industry, an army, and a navy capable of rivaling those of the great powers.

Scientists and engineers from the United States and Europe were invited to come to Japan to give lectures and teach classes in universities and schools where scientific and technical instruction was being developed. Japanese students went abroad to perfect their knowledge. The State encouraged this rapid modernization. It financed the building of Japan's first railroads and set up armament and ammunition factories. Wealthy traders and even samurais became directors of large industrial companies specializing in textiles, mechanical engineering, and ship-

In 1912 Tokyo celebrated the funeral of Mutsuhito, the emperor who made Japan the great power of Asia.

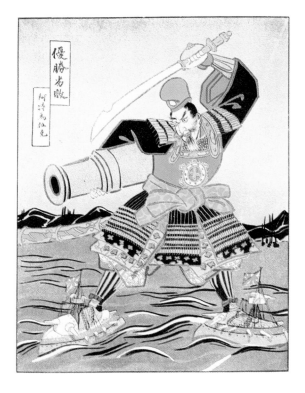

優勝劣敗

阿特馬拉克

building. They hired peasants who left the countryside and moved to cities on the east coast, where they worked long hours for low wages. Japanese products were cheap and therefore easy to export not only to neighboring Asian countries but also to Europe. There "Chinese ornaments," such as oriental vases, china, and embroidered fabrics manufactured in enormous quantities by Japanese industry, were the latest fashion.

The life of the Japanese changed on the outside. In cities, businessmen, the military, employees, and workers began to dress like Europeans. Once home, however, they took off their morning coats or suits, put on their kimonos, and participated in the tea ceremony with their wives, whose hair and dress was in the traditional style.

The emperor granted a Constitution. In principle, he no longer governed alone. A Chamber of Deputies had to represent the nation's will. However, it was elected by fewer than a million men, and the Japanese archipelago had 47 million inhabitants. Most Japanese looked upon their country as a large family with the emperor as the father. He was a father to whom advice could be given but who had to be obeyed. Yet Japan experienced serious problems. Its population was growing too rapidly, and not enough rice was produced to feed every mouth. Furthermore, the country had to import all its iron ore and a large share of

the coal needed by its industries. The numerous advisers in the emperor's circle thought that Japan had become powerful enough to take from the Asian continent what it could not find at home.

In 1895 the Japanese armies attacked China. They won such brilliant victories that the great powers began to worry — especially Russia, which had major interests in northern China. Nine years later, the world was dumbfounded when it heard that the Japanese had bombed and destroyed the Russian squadron controlling the harbor of Port Arthur in Manchuria without declaring war. It was the beginning of a terrible war between the Czar's troops and those of the "son of the Sun." A series of Japanese victories followed. On May 27, 1905, a Russian reinforcement fleet left the Baltic Sea to help the besieged Port Arthur. The Russian fleet was wiped out by Japanese guns on ships in the Tsushima Strait. Russia asked for peace and gave up its positions in Manchuria to Japan. Japan became one of the world's major powers whose armies no longer feared any adversary.

"In order to rule the world, one has to be strong." A French caricature of 1907 represents Japan as a giant samurai whose feet are battleships.

On May 27, 1905, the Russian fleet, after a long voyage from the Baltic Sea all the way to the coast of Korea, entered the Tsushima Strait. The Japanese closed the trap. One by one, the large Russian battleships were sent to the bottom of the ocean.

When Admiral Nebogatov decided to surrender, the disaster was total. Out of thirty-eight boats, only three escort ships managed to escape. All in all, 4,830 Russian sailors lost their lives. Admiral Togo's triumph was complete.

England in Transition

Victoria reigned as Queen of England from 1837 to 1901 and as Empress of India from 1876 to 1901. The old Queen was affectionately called "Granny" by her subjects.

"The love from all your sons surrounds you! The love from all your daughters reaches out to you! The love from your entire people supports you!" This was inscribed on one of the banners decorating the streets of every British town, when the English wanted to express the respect they had for Queen Victoria, who in 1897 celebrated her diamond jubilee. Sixty years of reign — sixty years during which Great Britain exercised undivided supremacy over Europe and over the rest of the world. At the turn of the century, however, Britain's supremacy was being challenged by powerful competitors.

England's spinning mills and weaving looms, coal mines, steel mills, and shipbuilding yards helped it to remain a major industrial power. The British navy was still the most powerful in the world and its ships transported nearly one third of the world's freight. The sumptuous building on Leadenhall street in London was a sign of the tremendous wealth possessed by Lloyd's, the largest insurance company in the world. The stock exchange and the large banks of London's financial district were the main indicators for the world's economy.

But English factories — many of them very old — manufactured costly products. Workers were often poorly paid and could not afford goods made at home. Instead, they bought foreign products on which the State did not levy any customs duties. In the face of this competition, many farmers gave up cultivating the land. The English imported more than half of what they ate! On foreign markets, the "German salesman" often took away business from his English colleague who had not encountered competition before.

Nevertheless, the English remained optimistic, for they were persuaded that God was particularly protective of their country. On the whole, the British — whether Anglican, Protestant, or Catholic — were faithful Christians and obeyed strict moral precepts. On Sundays the streets were empty and theaters and pubs were not allowed to open. The day was devoted to prayer and Bible reading. It was spent at home, a place honored and cherished by all "respectable" Englishmen, where the mother of the family reigned as an obedient spouse who protected the hearth.

Not every Englishman, however, had such a comfortable and happy life. A huge gap separated the refined gentleman living in the fashionable district of Chelsea in London from the person living in the slums. There squalor and misery reigned. The poorest people lived in workhouses, where they had to work to have food and a roof over their heads. England was a country where freedoms were recognized and where the government represented the entire country. Yet the right to vote, which for a long time was exclusively for a minority of landowners and rich people, had been granted to workers and farmers but not to poor people and servants.

Upon the death of Queen Victoria in 1901, her son Edward VII succeeded her. In 1906 he chose ministers who wanted to im-

The big cattle fair in Galway, Ireland, in 1913.

prove the lot of the least fortunate. Laws were enacted to create insurance programs against sickness and unemployment. In order to pay for this expenditure and maintain the enormous Royal Navy, the taxes of nobles and the rich upper class were greatly increased.

At the beginning of the century, Ireland represented a serious problem for the British. Inhabited by a majority of Catholics speaking Gaelic, the island was a very poor country controlled by English Protestant landowners. Ever since it had been united with England in 1800, many Irish people demanded their independence and organized deadly attacks against the English. Independence was to be obtained in 1921, when most of Ireland became a separate nation. However, in the northern part of the island, better known as Northern Ireland, a majority of Protestants have always wanted to remain part of England. All the elements for a civil war were present at the time and remain so to this day.

Even though all men had not obtained the right to vote in England at the turn of the century, women were demanding it loud and clear. The most determined, called "suffragettes," held demonstrations to make their cause known. Broken windows and attacks on the most strongly antifeminist deputies followed. But it was not until December 1918, that women in Great Britain went to the polls for the first time.

Edward VII, son of Victoria, became king at the age of sixty and reigned from 1901 to 1910.

Ludgate Circus in the "City of London," the financial district. The head offices of trading companies are housed in the buildings on the street over which the railroad bridge crosses.

Republican France

In 1901, Czar Nicolas II and the Czarina paid an official visit to France, where they were welcomed by Emile Loubet, president of the Republic. Since it had been signed in 1894, the Franco-Russian alliance continued to be a reason for celebration. Military parades, a visit by the Russian fleet to Toulon harbor, the building of the Alexander III bridge in Paris were all undertaken to glorify the alliance between the Republic, inheritor of the French Revolution, and the most authoritarian of sovereigns.

The plaster bust of Marianne — symbol of the French Republic — dominated the playground of the town school. That evening, after the children had gone home, the republican committee was holding an electoral meeting. Thirty years had gone by since Napoleon III's humiliating defeat by the Prussians and the proclamation of the Third Republic on September 4, 1870. During those thirty years, despite the loss of the provinces of Alsace and Lorraine, the Paris Commune, the royalists, plots, scandals, and assassination attempts by anarchists, the Republic managed to attract the devotion of most Frenchmen.

Universal suffrage gave the poor person's vote the same importance as the rich man's. Electing a deputy or the town council of a district had become an ordinary act that each adult male twenty-one or older took part in with dignity and respect. Since 1881, a law freed the press of all censorship. State education was free and compulsory and Republican teachers had the task of educating free citizens to take pride in their country.

Yet, at the turn of the century, the Third Republic experienced the greatest crisis in its history. It all started with the Dreyfus Affair. In 1894 Captain Alfred Dreyfus was accused of spying for Germany and was put on trial. He was sentenced to life imprisonment and deported to Devil's Island off the coast of what was then French Guiana. Dreyfus was a Jew and for those who read anti-Semitic newspapers, this fact alone was enough to condemn him! But for those who supported Dreyfus, such as his relatives and friends, there was no doubt as to his innocence. It turned out that the trial had been rigged. A letter written in a hand similar to his own had been enough to dishonor an officer.

On January 13, 1898, in the newspaper *L'Aurore*, the famous French writer Émile Zola published an open letter to the president of the Republic in which he denounced the errors and "crimes" committed by the Army and its desire to cover up the truth. Artists, scientists, and journalists took Dreyfus's side. With the same strength of conviction, others upheld that he was guilty "because a Jew can never be right in a court martial case or a matter involving the Honor of the Army!" "The Affair," as it was called at the time, caused dissension among families and lifelong friends. Buried hatreds were revived, especially toward those in favor of State education and those supporting Catholic education. Adversaries of the Republic, royalists, those in favor of military rule, or those just simply fed up with the numerous scandals sullying the regime, thought the time had come to take action.

Émile Loubet was in favor of a new trial. His election to the presidency of the Republic unleashed the fury of the nationalists, whose leader, Paul Déroulède, attempted to overthrow the government. It was a total failure. On June 4, 1899, during the "Grand Steeple" (horse race) at Auteuil, a group of young royalists attacked Loubet and crushed his top hat with their walking sticks. This did not, however, prevent Dreyfus's supporters from obtaining a second trial. The verdict was outrageous. Dreyfus was declared guilty with extenuating circumstances (the height of absurdity for a traitor!) and sentenced to 10 years imprisonment! On September 19 Loubet pardoned Dreyfus. But it was not until 1906 that Dreyfus was reinstated in the army as a major.

The "Republican defense" government decided to track down enemies of the regime. In 1901 a law on the freedom of association enabled the State to control religious orders which, through the voice of their newspapers, used the Dreyfus Affair to criticize the Republic. In 1902 elections brought an anticlerical majority to power. Priests were expelled and religious schools closed down. The law of December 9, 1905, proclaimed the separation of Church and State and deprived priests of the allowance paid to them by the government. Many were opposed to the law and chained themselves to church gates to prevent officials from drawing up a list of what the churches contained. In some towns, anticlerical mayors forbid processions and even the ringing of church bells! France was divided into two groups and only the threat of war in 1914 would restore the "sacred union" of its inhabitants.

On January 13, 1895, the newspaper Le Petit Journal *published this print entitled "The Traitor." A million readers thus had the impression of attending the public degradation of Captain Dreyfus in the courtyard at the Invalides in Paris. Nobody at that time believed in the innocence of the unfortunate officer.*

On September 22, 1900, President Loubet invited 22,000 French mayors to lunch to celebrate the proclamation of the First Republic in 1792. For this gigantic Republican feast, huge pavilions were set up in the Tuileries. Twelve chefs, 360 assistants and as many kitchen boys, 200 wine stewards, 700 head-waiters and 2,000 waiters were hired for the event. With the police contingent, 18,000 persons in all were busy feeding 22,000 others. Appetizers and hors d'oeuvres were followed by salmon, steak, duckling, poularde de Bresse, pheasant meat loaf, salad, ice cream, cheese, fruit, and petits fours. All this was washed down with 60,000 bottles of Bordeaux and 20,000 bottles of champagne, coffee, and liqueur. After the meal, each mayor went with a cigar in his mouth to visit the World's Fair!

The Second Reich

In the city of Essen, in the Ruhr valley, the gigantic Krupp armament plants were set up. Barges and trains transported iron ore and coke, which conveyor belts brought to the throat of blast furnaces. These large metallurgical enterprises enabled Germany to surpass Great Britan's steel production in 1903.

At the sound of the drum, the pupils of the Gymnasium (German High School) in Mannheim lined up in formation. One of them, Hans Werner, adjusted the cap of his uniform. He was seventeen years old in 1900 and in his last year of secondary school. In the following year, he was planning on attending the famous university of Heidelberg. He was still deciding between philosophy and history.

Hans was proud of his country, and of the great Reich whose Prussian king proclaimed himself emperor after his resounding victory over France in 1871. The kaiser William II governed Germany with an iron fist.

Germany's Chamber of Deputies, the Reichstag, was elected by popular vote, but it had little power. The military, composed for the most part of Prussians, along with numerous civil servants, helped the emperor govern as he saw fit. Under his leadership, Germany became the most modern country in Europe.

Hans could see the living proof. Day and night, barges sailed down the Rhine, unloading coal for the chemical factories in Ludwigshafen, whose smokestacks poured out a cloud of black smoke over the region. The farmers Hans knew had reason to be content. Their wheat and sugar beet crops doubled in twenty years, and their stables contained fat dairy cows.

The year before, Hans had been able to take advantage of a cruise down the Rhine with his parents to visit the Ruhr valley. He discovered the formidable power of Germany. More than two thousand miners worked there extracting coal from some of the world's largest coal mines. There were the steel factories and rolling mills of the Krupp and Thyssen plants, the docks in Duisburg, the workers to whom the Reich granted health insurance and a decent pension.

What fascinated Hans, however, was the

Optics was a modern industry in which the Germans excelled. Their high quality products were exported all over Europe.

KATALOGE GRATIS UND FRANKO

EMIL BUSCH, A.-G., OPTISCHE INDUSTRIE, RATHENOW

army. Every Sunday, soldiers, wearing gleaming pointed helmets, marched through the square of the Wasserturm (the water tower) in perfect order. The infantry preceded the gigantic "uhlans," brave horsemen who rode with spears in their hands on perfectly harnessed horses.

During the summer recess, students could be seen sitting at sidewalk cafés on the square, shouting and yelling. The slightest quarrel was settled by a sword duel, which the officers were more than happy to arbitrate. Hans envied them. He dreamed of being able to walk around with a scar on his face, proof of courage and manliness.

Among the teachers at the school, old Grübber was the one who had the most influence on the students. His courses were a permanent tribute to the genius of the German people. Was Wagner not one of the greatest musicians of the century? Did Nietzsche not revolutionize philosophy by proposing a heroic and violent ideal to men? When Grübber explained the history of his country, his hands began to move in all directions and his face lit up. "How could the Alsatians, Danes, and Poles, integrated into the Reich, refuse German culture? Luckily the kaiser will know how to put these rebels back in their place!"

Under William II, Germany adopted an aggressive policy of colonial expansion. In 1898 Admiral von Tirpitz decided that Germany needed a powerfully armed navy. This caused concern in England. The Reich allied itself with Austria-Hungary and Italy, which both shared the same ambitions. The State appropriated an increasingly large amount of money each year for the purchase of equipment· to outfit the most modern, powerful, and best commanded army in the world. Like all the other large countries in Europe, Germany stated that it was only looking for peace — and prepared for war.

William II, dressed in a white uniform and wearing a helmet on which is perched the German eagle, presides over a military inspection in Hamburg. The Kaiser was chief of the army. Always surrounded by officers, he kept a close watch over the army to ensure that it was permanently ready for war. It was the pride of a State created on the battlegrounds.

Along the Danube

I n the early morning hours, the passengers on the *Orient Express*, which had left Paris the night before, were still sleeping in their luxurious sleeping compartments when the most famous train in Europe crossed the border between Germany and Austria. In a short while through the train's misted windows, they would see the peaceful snow-covered villages and the large towns huddled around their picturesque onion-shaped church towers.

In the evening they would be in Vienna, capital of the Austro-Hungarian empire. The great city of nearly two million inhabitants seemed to live by the same rhythm as Strauss's waltzes. The large Ring, or major boulevard surrounding the old city, was a succession of theaters, opera houses, restaurants, and cafés. Nobles and the rich upper class built beautiful homes there. Parties and festivals were being held all the time. The most famous boulevard was the Prater, which drew all of Europe's upper crust during Mardi Gras. Famous for its artists, Vienna was also known the world over for its scientists, its university, and its school of medicine which had several thousand students.

But the "beautiful blue Danube" that graced the city also flowed through Hungary, Serbia, Bulgaria, and Romania. Nicknamed the "powder keg of Europe" by newspapermen of the time, this area comprised over twenty peoples with different languages and nationalities. Hatreds and ill feelings, accumulated over the centuries, could be reignited at any moment. The old Francis Joseph ruled over this patchwork as emperor of Austria and king of Hungary. Each country had its own government and parliament, but there was only one army for the entire Austro-Hungarian empire.

Vienna and the square in front of the opera house. This is where the capital's high society met.

The imperial couple of Austria and the king and queen of Hungary, Francis Joseph and Elisabeth attended on June 8, 1896, the celebration of the thousand year anniversary of the entry of Hungarian hordes to the territory to which they gave their name. Members of the clergy and representatives of the diet in Budapest came to pay tribute to their sovereigns.

In Austria, the Germans dominated. They outnumbered all the other nationalities combined (Czechs, Poles, Italians). Around Prague, capital of the Czech-inhabited province of Bohemia, mines and factories developed. Aware of the fact that they belonged to the empire's richest region, the Czechs wanted to turn the area into a State as independent as Hungary.

Unlike Austria, Hungary was mainly an agricultural country. Hungarians, who formed a majority, made their language, Magyar, compulsory in all schools. The other peoples of the country — Slovaks, Croatians, Romanians — did not accept the Hungarians' authoritarian rule and demanded their autonomy.

This continual bickering and quarreling between nationalities could even be seen in the Austro-Hungarian army, where Hungarian soldiers and officers refused to obey orders given in German unless they were translated into Magyar!

For Francis Joseph, the situation was serious. His empire was on the verge of bursting at the seams. To make matters worse, the small kingdom of Serbia south of the Danube dreamed of creating a great State comprised of all the Slavs in the south. It wanted a "Yugoslavia." In order to avoid this danger, in 1908 the empire annexed Bosnia-Herzegovina, a former province of the Turkish Empire inhabited by Serbians. This annexation did not please the people living there. Secret organizations supported by the king of Serbia decided to organize resistance against the Austrians by preparing attacks and plotting the assassination of members of the imperial family.

Czar Nicholas II dressed in cavalry uniform caracoles at the head of his army staff. A world separated this pretty post card used as propaganda from the reality of the Russian army which, despite the impressive number of soldiers it could mobilize, did not have modern equipment. Its leaders failed to realize the inferiority separating it from its European rivals.

The Last Czar

"*Sire! Over three hundred thousand of us are present here today, but we are only men in appearance. Whoever dares raise his voice to defend the interests of workers is thrown into prison or sent into exile…*

Sire! Is this in accordance with the divine laws which grant you the power to rule?

Are not all workers of Russia better off dying?

Sire! Do not refuse your protection to your people. Rid your reign of the arbitrary, poverty, ignorance."

On Sunday, January 9, 1905, in St. Petersburg, a huge crowd gathered in front of the Winter Palace. People had come to present this petition to Nicolas II, czar of all Russians. Nicolas II had been crowned in 1894. He reigned over an empire of 120 million inhabitants. Money invested by the English, Belgians, and especially the French in Russian companies had made it possible to build railroads and large factories. But Russia was far from being a modern country. There were more than 100 million peasants, and only forty years had passed since serfdom had been abolished, making them free men. Yet, most of them, known as "moujiks" in Russian, were poor and still under the power of "barines," their former masters. Illiterate and poverty-stricken, they led periodic revolts, burning the castles and farms of nobles and "koulaks," nouveau riche peasants whom they abhorred. The moujiks demanded the distribution of land among the peasants. The czar replied with a bloody repression and deportations to work camps.

The workers, who barely numbered five million, were not much better off than the peasants. They earned extremely poor wages and lived near the factories in ghetto-like neighborhoods. They worked twelve

In the taiga, the building of the Trans-Siberian Railroad mobilized tens of thousands of workers. Many were sentenced prisoners, deported to Siberia.

hours a day, six days a week.

Nicholas II thought colonizing Asia was a solution to Russia's problems. He had railroads built to Turkestan, but the most famous project was the Trans-Siberian Railroad, which in 1904 enabled traveling from Moscow to Vladivostok in ten days. But his ambitions met with Japanese opposition, which crushed the Russian army in 1905.

Despite these difficulties and the czar's disastrous policies, the crowd in St. Petersburg still believed in the emperor. "He is the father of the people...He is misled by evil advisers and ministers....He will do something to change the situation..." He did just that. After three warning shots, the army, stationed in front of the palace, opened fire on the bewildered crowd. Men, women, and children ran in all directions, easy targets in the white snow. It was a massacre with more than one thousand victims. January 9, 1905, came to be known in the annals of history as Red Sunday. A revolution ensued and shook up the entire country. Peasants revolted in the countryside. There were uprisings in the Asian provinces, strikes in factories, and even mutinies in the army. In Odessa, the large port on the Black Sea, the seamen on the battleship *Potemkine* took the workers' side.

Repression was not enough to restore calm. Boards of workers and peasants called "soviets" took over local power. Overwhelmed, the czar was forced to give in and promise reforms and grant freedoms. Once order had been restored, Nicolas II forgot his promises. He dismissed the deputies whose elections he had accepted in 1905. His police force tracked down political opponents, who were imprisoned or deported to Siberia. The upper class and even certain nobles believed the situation had to change, but they still hoped the czar would be able to transform the country and give up his absolute power. A few revolutionary groups, determined to take violent action, organized terrorist attacks against ministers, policemen, and military officials. They wanted to assassinate the czar just as his grandfather Alexander II had been in 1881. Others preferred to wait for a more favorable moment before fomenting a great revolution. To them, 1905 was a "rehearsal," and the next uprising would be for good. It would take place twelve years later.

Red Sunday. Gathered in front of the Winter Palace, the crowd began to run, the soldiers took aim, and an officer gave the signal to fire. Within a few seconds, Nicolas II lost the confidence of his people.

Moscow in 1900: Behind the red brick wall of the Kremlin rose the onion-shaped towers of the cathedral of the Assumption. Birthplace of the dynasty of czars, Moscow lost, to the benefit of St. Petersburg, its status as capital at the beginning of the eighteenth century. With 1,050,000 inhabitants, however, Moscow remained the most populated city in the empire.

Ильинскія ворота.
Porte Ilynskija.

Москва.
Moscou.

Constantinople. This picture of the bridge over the Golden Horn was taken in 1913 from the Galata section of the city. In the background are steamships and behind them Asia.

The End of an Empire

In this caricature, the inhabitants of countries surrounding Turkey strip the sultan Abdul-Hamid of his possessions. A Greek steals his cap, on which the word Crete is written. A Bulgarian carries off his saber, while an Austrian takes off his boots, which represent Bosnia and Herzegovina. The caricaturist of the newspaper (Le Pèlerin of October 18, 1908) had added the caption: "Luckily, I have a good constitution; maybe they'll leave me my shirt?"

Constantinople, the gateway to Asia! A foreigner just coming out of the central station would be struck by the pungent odors of the sea and grilled fish and by the incessant noise of shouting and yelling in a countless number of languages and dialects.

In 1900, 1,150,000 people lived in Constantinople (modern-day Istanbul) a city that spread over both sides of the Golden Horn, a deep gulf on the European bank of the Bosporus. This narrow arm of sea linked the Black Sea with the Sea of Marmara. Churches of all religions, mosques with their minarets reaching up to the sky, and sumptuous palaces surrounded by wooden houses reflected the diversity of peoples over which Abdul-Hamid II, sultan since 1876, ruled.

The Ottoman Empire was no longer the splendid power that had controlled the Mediterranean Sea from the sixteenth to the eighteenth century. Muslim Turks had been forced to grant independence to the Christians in the Balkans, who were supported by the major European countries. Greece, Serbia, Romania, and Bulgaria were thus created out of the remains of an empire whose influence had been so great that it was once referred to as the "Sublime Gate." Now it was no more than Europe's "sick man."

Taking advantage of this decline, Great Britain and France imposed their protectorate on Egypt and Tunisia. For more than four centuries these two countries had recognized the Turkish sultan as suzerain. But Abdul-Hamid was also caliph and therefore the religious leader of the Muslim community. He decided to make Christians pay for the humiliations his empire had been subjected to by the Western powers. Between 1894 and 1896, he let Kurdish Muslims massacre 200,000 Christian Armenians.

European journalists roused the indignation of their readers with stories of the "Turkish atrocities." Western governments threatened to intervene. The sultan had to accept the presence of foreign policemen sent to protect Christians and promised reforms that never came about. But the cruelty of Abdul-Hamid — the "red sultan," as he was known — increased as his power diminished. He borrowed large sums of money from English and French banks, but in order to reimburse his debts he was obliged to allow foreign bankers to collect sales taxes on tobacco, salt, alcohol, and stamps.

A German company assumed the task of building the railroad that was to link Constantinople to Baghdad. All the equipment, including the tracks, locomotives, and carriages, would be German. The company received a strip of land 12 miles wide for the entire length of the road bed with the right to exploit all its resources. In addition, the Turkish government was to pay the equivalent of 430,000 francs at the time for each mile of track laid!

Students and the military condemned the sultan's policy and accused him of selling out to the foreigners. The revolution of "young Turks" overthrew Abdul-Hamid in 1909 and replaced him with his brother Mehemet, who let them govern in his place. Admirers of Germany, they sought its alliance in an attempt to oppose the other European powers.

It was too late, however. In 1912 Italy took advantage of the empire's weakness and stole Libya from it after a deadly war. It was the last of its African possessions. Meanwhile, Greece, Serbia, and Bulgaria united and chased the Turks out of the Balkans.

In 1914 the Ottoman Empire's last remaining possessions in Europe consisted of Constantinople and a few cities between the Dardanelles and the Bosporus. In Asia, Arabs in Syria, Jordan, and Palestine and Christians in Lebanon dreamed of setting up independent States out of the ruins of the Ottoman Empire.

A bachi-bouzouk was a fearsome soldier responsible for keeping order in the Christian countries of the Ottoman Empire.

Jerusalem in 1900: Within the heart of the esplanade of the old temple, enclosed by the wall built under King Herod, the golden dome of Omar's mosque is proof of the holiness of the place for the Muslim religion as well as the Jewish and Christian religions.

The American Adventure

The "Model T" Ford was the first automobile to be built on an assembly line. This light car was produced on a large scale (from 1908 to 1927, 15 million "Model Ts" rolled out of Ford factories) and was less expensive than any of the cars produced by its competitors. The automobile industry grew into an important activity in the United States. It was not long before Henry Ford was ousted as America's top car manufacturer. In 1912 W.C. Durant bought the trademarks Buick, Cadillac, and Chevrolet, which he grouped together into one single firm. The name of the company was General Motors. Since that time, his enterprise has remained the world's largest manufacturer of automobiles.

"American factories produce more than the American people can use; American land produces more than its population can consume. Fate has defined our policy; world trade has to be and will be ours...We will set up trading posts all over the world as centers of distribution for American products. We will build a navy as strong as our country...

Our institutions will carry the star spangled banner on the wings of commerce. And American law, American order, and American civilization will be sown in areas which up until now have only known violence and obscurantism..." Senator Albert Beveridge's speech in Boston on April 27, 1898, ended in a thunder of applause. He had just expressed the pride of a wealthy and powerful nation that was looking for new opportunities to expand its frontiers. A week had gone by since the United States had declared war on Spain. American soldiers had landed in Cuba and Puerto Rico, while the fleet of Admiral Dewey was crossing the Pacific to take possession of the Philippines.

The United States was already the world's major power. The Civil War, waged between 1861 and 1865, was no more than a painful memory. The Far West had been entirely conquered. The transcontinental railroad had linked the East to the West since 1869, and pioneers were now farming

vast areas of land.

The Indian revolts had been quelled in a blood bath. Three hundred thousand survivors lived penned in reservations on the poorest land. The great Apache chief Geronimo was exiled in Florida and peacefully spent the rest of his days as a farmer converted to Christianity. Buffalo Bill, the famous cowboy who killed buffaloes in the 1880s, was a music-hall star who recreated the Wild West on stages the world over.

The American adventure was now that of big business and industry. Coal mines in the Appalachians produced more coal than did English mines. Huge open pits supplied iron ore transported by barges over the Great Lakes and canals to the blast furnaces of Pittsburgh, the steel capital of the United States. Oil, which had been discovered in Pennsylvania, was now flowing from the ground in California and Texas. In 1894 there was a gold rush to Alaska, where rich veins of the ore had been discovered.

Businessmen amassed huge fortunes. From rags to riches, they became kings of steel, railroads, and oil. They were the true heroes of the time. Their law was the same as that of the Far West: "Every one has his time, but woe to the loser!"

Open to talent and hard work, American society was not always kind to the losers. In the Southern states, the United States' Constitution, which recognized racial equality and gave blacks the right to vote in 1865, was not applied. Whites did not allow blacks to vote unless they could read and explain the laws of the state in which they lived, whereas illiterate whites were able to vote. Bars, restaurants, train cars, and schools were barred to blacks. Marriages between whites and blacks were forbidden. The United States Supreme Court, the highest judicial authority in the nation, did not condemn this segregation.

ON THE 'HIGHWAY' IN THE FAMOUS BURK-WAGGONER OIL POOL

The black gold rush. Discovered in Texas during the last twenty years of the nineteenth century, oil brought great wealth to Texan farmers lucky enough to see the "black gold" gush forth from their fields. Derricks sprang up and attracted businessmen like John D. Rockefeller, who controlled the transport and refining of oil. Small producers were forced to sell off their entire production at a price fixed by the companies.

The most racist Southern whites met in secret societies which the Federal government attempted in vain to outlaw. The most famous of these societies was the Ku Klux Klan. Its members dressed in long white gowns and wore hoods over their heads to hide their faces. They terrorized their victims and sometimes even went so far as to lynch them.

Workers and small farmers, who were victims of a decline in wages and farm prices, formed groups and demanded reforms. Theodore Roosevelt, who was elected president in 1901, defended their cause. Through his efforts, most of the forty-six states adopted laws reducing the workday to eight hours. Child labor was outlawed for those under the age of twelve.

Roosevelt fought the huge trusts which wielded so much power that they could buy off politicians to support their interests in Congress. To oppose them, he invoked the Sherman Anti-Trust Act of 1890 and also created national parks to protect America's wildlife from encroaching industry. He vigorously championed the rights of the "little man" and denounced "malefactors of great wealth."

The Triumph of Capitalism

This caricature from 1890 denounced the power of the railway-transport trust. Jay Gould, known as the king of railroads, is depicted as a puppeteer who controls everything by manipulating his puppets. He dominated the major railroads that linked the East Coast to the Middle West. At his feet, a sign reads "All freight seeking the seaboard MUST pass here and pay any tolls we demand."

The building of cities, railroads, and factories and the digging of canals all required huge amounts of capital. Gold and silver coins were no longer enough. All over the world, specialized banks printed paper bills whose designated value could be immediately exchanged by tellers for an equivalent sum in gold coins. Everyone could therefore place his trust in the paper money and accept it as payment, just like coins. Checks were still rare and used only by the rich to pay large sums. Credit enabled shopowners to pay for goods they sold to their customers at a later date. Because of the new system, it was no longer necessary to be rich to open a store or a workshop. Everyone was free to start his own business!

But in order to set up a large company, credit was not enough. Money was usually found by dividing the amount of capital needed into small portions called shares or stocks. Each share represented a part of the company and could be sold on a special market known as the stock exchange or stock market. People who purchased stock became part owners in the company. Each year, they received their share of the company's profit in the form of a dividend.

Bankers offered investors the possibility of increasing their savings through the purchase of bonds. A bond is an interest-bearing certificate issued by a government or business, promising to pay the holder a specified sum of money on a specified date. Through the sale of bonds, state and local governments were able to raise capital funds at a lower interest rate. The holders of these bonds received a small yield, but their investment was guaranteed by the state or municipality. "Safe investments" like these, however, could not ensure a rapid fortune. Many speculators preferred buying stocks in the hope that they would be able to resell them a few months later at a higher price. Some became rich, but others were ruined when businesses failed.

In order to increase their profits, large companies waged a vicious battle, using every trick they could. Two firms wanting to elbow out a competitor might agree to lower their prices, even if it meant selling at a loss! They then bought the shares, machines, and factories of their unfortunate rival. As for the workers and employees, they could go elsewhere!

Using these methods, businessmen in the United States were able to control more than half the oil refining activity, steel production, and railway traffic in an entire region. They could impose their high prices and tariffs. Free competition no longer existed!

In order to restore this freedom, which is the basis of capitalism, the American government passed antitrust legislation in 1890, forbidding such practices. But through banks owned by these companies, the trusts purchased huge quantities of stocks and managed to retain their monopolies.

For large companies and banks, the world was a huge market lacking in capital for development. These banks proposed loans to the governments of the world's poorest countries, such as China, the Turkish Empire, and even Russia, in exchange for the right to collect taxes in the form of customs duties or to exploit mineral resources. And, increasingly, they asked their own governments to support their interests through the intervention of their ambassadors, ministers and, if necessary, their soldiers.

Capitalism had become a weapon, a double-edged sword capable of leading Europe into war.

This is a stock certificate from a Belgian company operating blast furnaces in the Donets Basin in the Ukraine, southern Russia.

From 1896 to 1906, the discovery of gold in the Klondike in Alaska drew adventurers in search of fortune. Mining conditions were terrible, especially in winter. In this picture, a gold digger is sifting gold-bearing sand with a rudimentary machine.

The Middle Class

A bourgeois interior during the Belle Époque. The green plant sits imposingly on the Chinese-inspired tripod in a Chinese-like vase. The "modern-style" table must be a recent purchase. Comfort meant accumulating trinkets, mantle objects, small paintings, and of course an upright piano like the one being played by the young girl of the house.

Great beneficiaries of the Industrial Revolution, the middle class, or bourgeoisie, as they were sometimes referred to, dominated the Belle Époque. Who were the bourgeoisie, the middle class? Did they have a lot of money? Were they rich landowners? Owners of businesses? The bourgeoisie were people who earned their living in businesses and professions rather than by the work of their hands. This very broad definition describes the middle class as a whole but does not take into account differences within the class.

At the top of society were the wealthy upper middle class. They were comprised of bankers, big industrialists, and merchants who shared the same easy, gilded life as the aristocracy with whom they were often united through marriage. They lived in private mansions or large apartment buildings in wealthy neighborhoods. Their drawing rooms were open to famous celebrities of the time, world-renowned doctors, illustrious writers, and artists. They were the main clientele of plush seaside resorts, cruise ships, and luxurious trains.

Conservative in their tastes and often in their political views, the upper middle class pretended to lead a sober and sensible life. They were against overindulgence, except perhaps at the table, for meals during the Belle Époque defied all the rules of proper nutrition.

Upper middle-class wives stayed home and managed the household. They saw to it that their staff of servants, from cook to chambermaid, carried out their specific tasks. They looked after the upbringing of their children from an early age, before handing their daughters over to expensive boarding schools. Parents were often the only ones to decide on the future of their children. For their sons, difficult studies were necessary so that they could take over their father's business or profession. Suitable candidates were chosen for their young daughters who, nine times out of ten, married the first young man they were presented to.

Doctors, businessmen, persons with small private incomes, and attorneys were all members of a middle class whose importance became considerable. Though not rich, they were well off. Not very attracted to luxury, which they felt they could not afford, nor to splendor, which they considered useless, they placed work and savings at the top of their list of values and virtues. They employed only an "all-around" maid and only allowed their wives to indulge in elegant fashions when they went to balls, the theater, or the opera, where watching and listening were not as important as being seen!

Democracy and universal male suffrage enabled members of the middle class to enter politics, in which they placed all their energy and talents. Believers in reason and progress, which they felt they embodied, they upheld ideas opposed to those of the old nobility, who were allied with the rich upper class. They were in favor of a school system that allowed all children, especially their own, access to high-ranking offices.

The lower middle class — office employees, shop clerks, subordinate civil servants — earned little more than workers' households where both spouses worked. But they belonged to another world, spoke another language, adopted the same manners, fashions, attitudes, and leisure activities as the bourgeoisie. To them, living in a bourgeois manner meant living without worries, paying their rent on time, not going to the same cafés as workers, reading a newspaper "like it should be read," wearing a hat and not a cap, a hard collar and a tie, and not having debts. For those who were lucky enough to benefit from a few days' vacation, it meant resting at the seaside, in the mountains, or at a thermal spa.

J. Béraud, a recognized and admired painter at the time of the Belle Époque, painted the rue du Havre in Paris when school was being let out at the Lycée Condorcet. A strict code of dress showed they belonged to the respectable middle class. All women wore hats. A woman without one could only be seen in a workers' neighborhood. Children wore short trousers, long socks, a cap, and a cape. Adolescent boys adopted the dressing style of their fathers. The only extravagance in dress tolerated by the middle-class male was the boater, a straw hat that in summer replaced the derby hat.

A London slum in 1909. The workers' dwellings were overpopulated and looked onto a narrow inner courtyard. In these areas, tuberculosis spread like wildfire.

The Mine and the Factory

One by one, the miners, wearing hats and carrying lamps, piled into an iron cage-like elevator. Every day stripped to the waist because the heat was unbearable, they went to work 1300 feet underground. They dug huge quantities of coal, which they tore from the earth with pickaxes. Industry required increasingly large amounts of fuel to operate its steam engines, transform its metals, and produce gas for heat.

From the green valleys in Wales to the dreary stretches in northern France, from the banks of the Ruhr to the hollows of the Appalachians, the mine transformed the countryside. Coal tips, or artificial hills made from waste left over from the coal mines, dominated the area where pitheads indicated the place of each mine shaft. Rows of small identical houses ran geometrically along the streets, whose names bore the shaft number where their inhabitants worked. The mine commanded, controlled, and ruled over everything. The men, women, and children were housed by the mining company, baptized and married in the church it built, and educated in its school. They had no other horizon to look to than a life of underground work with the ever-present fear of an accident.

The flooding and collapse of a gallery were constant risks. But what the miner feared most was the "firedamp explosion." This was an explosion of inflammable gas capable of causing fatal catastrophes. On March 10, 1906, in the small mining town of Courrières in the Pas-de-Calais, France, a fire killed 1,219 men! To keep production from decreasing, the company made miners go down to work, despite the accident that had already occurred! The burial of the victims turned into a riot. Forty-six thousand miners went on strike and threatened to deprive France of coal. The government sent 25,000 soldiers in to restore order. After two months of no wages and the risk of losing their homes, the "blackfaces" went back to work, seething with anger.

Located near the coal mines, steelworks and chemical factories operated day and night. Coal was roasted in big coke ovens, stripped of its tar and gas and carried through miles of pipes to gasometers. These were gigantic reservoirs built on the outskirts of large cities. At the foot of the blast furnaces where the burning coke melted the iron ore, a continuous flow of pig iron was directed toward converters, which transformed it into steel. Railroad tracks, sheet metal, and cables were produced in huge quantities and at increasingly lower prices.

The assembly of a ship in a French shipyard at the turn of the century.

Huge buildings constructed with metal beams housed immense workshops employing several thousand workers. Giant power hammers, 60 feet high and weighing 50 tons, crashed down on glowing metal bars or plates which, after repeated blows, gradually assumed the form of a propeller shaft or blade.

But these men whose work ensured the economy's growth and their employers' profits lived in conditions not to be envied. In large cities, the arrival of an ever larger number of newcomers made rents climb. The rent for a tiny dwelling without gas or running water ate up one third of a worker's income. Women were often forced to find jobs in spinning or weaving mills, where little skill was required. Their wages were very low. While a metal worker earned 5 francs a day, a woman hired in the textile sector received only 1 franc. This was equivalent to the price of four pounds of bread and a quart of milk! Others did piece work at home and were paid on a per-item basis or found jobs in middle-class families cleaning houses and washing clothes.

For most of the labor force, what some called the Belle Époque was a ten- or twelve-hour workday. It was a life without vacations or trips — a life in which sickness and accidents often led to poverty and tragedy.

Child labor was regulated in the major industrial countries. It was forbidden to employ children under fourteen years of age in American mines. Nevertheless, a 1900 census reveals that 14,000 underage children worked in the coal mines of Pennsylvania. They worked ten hours a day sorting coal.

At the beginning of the century, Jean Jaurès embodied European socialism. The great speaker defended the dignity of workers in his speeches. Founder of the newspaper L'Humanité, he put it to the service of the young French Socialist party, created in 1905. A tireless pilgrim of peace, he unrelentlessly denounced the risks of a war, which he accused capitalists of wanting to start. He died on July 31, 1914, assassinated by a nationalist fanatic.

May 1st, 1900

"Eight hours work, eight hours free time, eight hours sleep!" In all the world's large industrial cities, processions bearing red flags and banners were held in the streets. Since 1899, May 1st had become an international day of protest. On that day, hundreds of thousands of workers did not go to work. Instead they demonstrated for better living conditions, shorter working hours, higher wages.

On their banners, a few slogans summed up their action: "Solidarity, strength through unity!..." Unity was a great problem for workers in the nineteenth century. In a society that pretended to be free, how could one demand a decent salary if someone else agreed to work for close to nothing? Was the employer not free to hire whomever he wanted and pay him as he saw fit? The worker was also free to accept or refuse. It was against this reasoning that trade unions reacted.

As early as 1830, trade unions in England offered to protect workers against the upper class, the "useless and idle part of society." Tolerated in Great Britain, trade unions came up against hostility from governments that supported the interests of employers. In France, strikes were offenses punishable by law and were not authorized until 1864. It was not until 1884 that French law allowed workers to join trade unions! And yet, how many workers known for having led strikes or belonging to a trade union were systematically refused work by employers intent on not giving in to any of the workers' demands?

Nevertheless, at the beginning of the century, the number of trade-union members continued to increase. Over two million Britons were militant members, as many Germans joined worker organizations, a million and a half Americans defended their rights in the A.F.L. (American Federation of Labor). In France less than five hundred thousand Frenchmen were scattered over a multitude of trade organizations, which the General Confederation of Labor had been trying to regroup since 1895.

English, American, and German trade unions were of the opinion that it would be possible to obtain major reforms without changing society. In contrast, in France, Italy, and Spain, revolutionary tendencies were appearing and trade unionism and strikes were viewed as ways of overthrowing "the bourgeois state" and replacing it with a social republic led by workers.

In the United States, the Women's Auxiliary Typographical Union demonstrated for an eight-hour work day.

Progress in the area of democracy with universal suffrage gave workers greater political weight. In 1889 the International Socialist movement was created with the aim of bringing together Socialist parties from all over the world.

In England, the Labour party had been representing trade unions in Parliament since 1906. Its leaders, who only wanted to improve workers' rights, did not question either the monarchy or society.

The German Social Democrats formed the largest Socialist party in the world. They owned newspapers with widespread circulations, controlled the powerful trade unions and through them demanded the application of reforms. In the elections of 1903, they obtained 30 percent of the German vote. The emperor William II tolerated them as long as they did not attempt to overthrow his government. He also feared that repression would lead to revolution.

Much less numerous than the Germans, French socialists were also more divided. Some defended ideas advocated by Karl Marx in his writings. They wanted to take power by force, confiscate factories and large landholdings, and set up a socialist state. Others limited their demands to reforms and were of the opinion, expressed by their great speaker Jean Jaurès, that the Republic would be able to grant workers the dignity and rights they deserved. However, Jaurès especially wanted all the Socialist parties and trade unions in Europe to be capable of mobilizing themselves in order to prevent the various governments from declaring war. United through the same work, the same concerns, the same demands, and as members of one single organization, the workers of Europe would form a solid front against anyone who opposed them.

In August 1908, a twenty-four hour strike by Paris workers turned into a confrontation. Facing the police, the strikers defended the entry to the rue du Château d'Eau. Trade unions had built the Labor Stock Exchange whose rooms were used for their meetings. At the windows of the building, strikers wave the red flag of revolt and the black flag of anarchy — at the time symbols of the French trade-union movement.

The City's Changing Face

The first skyscraper built in Tokyo in 1890. This 12-story building had the first elevator ever installed in Japan. It was located in the center of an amusement park where the Japanese came for one of their favorite pastimes — flying kites.

A telephone exchange in Paris in 1904. In order to reach someone by telephone, the caller would first have to go through one of the telephone operators shown here.

At the beginning of the twentieth century, the city was the mirror of progress. It offered work, money, entertainment, and the promise of a better life to anyone who wanted the adventure. Every day a flow of farm workers arrived, leaving behind their harsh and monotonous life in the countryside. They were determined to have a piece of the pie. In industrial regions, new cities sprang up like mushrooms around mines and factories.

The faces of old cities changed. The time-worn houses in old city centers disappeared under the picks and shovels of demolition crews. Large avenues radiated out from town squares. When evening fell, they were illuminated by gas lamps. New and beautiful six- and seven-story buildings offered their occupants the latest in comfort — running water, gas, and even electricity. The most luxurious apartments had elevators and their own bathrooms.

In capitals and major cities, specialized business and shopping districts attracted thousands of employees, sales clerks, and customers during the day. With improved public transportation, they were now able to move freely from place to place. Electric trolleys and even subways in New York, Berlin, London, and Paris gradually replaced horse omnibuses.

In Paris, regulations were passed forbidding the dumping of household rubbish in the streets. In 1883 a man named Poubelle, who was prefect in Paris, imposed the use of trash cans. In 1894 all new buildings had to be connected to a central sewerage system. This system was an underground city and a true replica of the city above. Its tunnels were named after the streets above, and miles of water pipes, gas lines, and electric and telephone cables ran along its walls. It also had a network of air tubes that made it possible to send urgent letters by compressed air.

Modernization, however, was costly. In city centers, the price of land was so high

Paris 1900: Metro workers in front of the fountain on the Place Saint-Michel are building a steel tunnel that will be lowered into a 66-foot deep ditch. It will pass under the bed of the Seine River.

that only large firms, banks and insurance companies could afford to put up new buildings.

Progress and modernization also contributed to the creation of two cities in one. Living around parks and gardens, the inhabitants of "nice neighborhoods" did not see factories or smell their smoke. The only poor people they tolerated near them were their servants. Forced to live on the industrial outskirts or in the inner-city neighborhoods deserted by the middle class, workers and craftsmen formed a world apart, with their own language, traditions, and customs. Such a world was Harlem in New York and Le Marais in Paris. This was a world the middle class feared would be the cause of uprisings — a world over which the police kept a careful watch. Though the working class had helped to build the city, they were far from being able to take advantage of all its benefits. Their neighborhoods still retained certain trades — mending bowls and china, selling rags, sewing and repairing clothing. And they kept their public washing places. There women did their laundry together and had their public baths and showers, which at the end of the week attracted a long line of workers impatient to feel clean again before putting on their white Sunday shirts.

The Flatiron Building in New York. This 17-story metal structure, in the shape of a triangle (flatiron) was begun in 1899 and completed in 1902. It affords the best views of three streets of Manhattan — Broadway, Fifth Avenue, and Twenty-third Street.

The wine harvest in Saint-Émilion at the beginning of the century. The wine harvest remains true to tradition. Wooden baskets are carried to the wine press by an ox.

Fenaison near La Tour-d'Auvergne (Puy-de-Dôme). This photograph, taken in 1911, is a traditional image of the French countryside. Women with large bonnets gather up grass reaped by the men beforehand.

Country Life

The shining plowshare cut through the heavy soil, lifted and turned to either side of the furrow by the moldboard. Behind the two powerful and peaceful oxen steadily pulling the plow, the farm hand leaned with all his weight on the handles. He rose with the sun and his life was based on the rhythm of work in the fields. The fear of a devastating storm or a late frost, the hope of a good crop or an abundant wine harvest were his main concerns.

In the countryside, the Industrial Revolution and the century of progress had not greatly modified ways of living or thinking.

Despite the steam engine, which could be found on farms in Western Europe and the United States, the countryside managed to feed a growing population using the force of animals and the sweat of men. Except for England and Germany, more men worked in agriculture than in industry or trade. In America, millions of pioneers settled in the Midwest on the prairie. They planted wheat and raised huge herds of cattle. In Europe the exodus from the country to the city had still not emptied the countryside, where it was said farm hands were lacking.

The farmhouse, village, and small town nearby formed a setting that the farm hand rarely left, except to serve his mandatory term in the army. This was considered to be the great adventure of his life. It was then that he discovered the existence of a world other than his own, where houses were not all alike, where people had a strange accent and did not understand his dialect. He felt lost in surroundings where it was "everyone for himself." How different from a world where everyone knew everyone else!

In the village, houses were often inhabited by three generations. In the evening, at dinnertime, everyone sat at a designated spot. At the end of the large table was the head of the house. He sat with his back turned toward the warm fireplace and was served first. Around him were his sons or sons-in-law, who talked only when it was their turn. They made sure they did not contradict him. The women and girls served the men and sat down to eat only when the men's plates were filled and the small children were in bed. After supper, the family gathered around the fireplace and talked about work, animals, and crops. When only the immediate family was present, and there was no danger of being overheard by a stranger, talk turned to buying a piece of land. The family was prepared to make any sacrifice to increase the size of their farm with fertile land, which would remain in the family throughout future generations.

In the most developed nations, farms began to show improvements. In the small towns, there were agricultural contests to select the most beautiful specimens of livestock; and seed merchants sold seeds that ensured better yields. With the introduction of fertilizers, the land no longer had to recuperate by laying fallow. Clover and alfalfa were sown, making it possible to feed larger

herds. The mechanical reaper pulled by horses did more work than twenty robust men, but the cut ears of wheat had to be bound together into sheafs and loaded into oxcarts. This was a job that still had to be done by hand. With the invention of the steam threshing machine, men no longer had to flail down rhythmically on just-harvested wheat.

Farmers acquired new ways of life. An iron cooking stove replaced the open fireplace, and a wool mattress took the place of straw on which they slept. Gas lamps now lit the farms instead of candles. The suit worn by the farmer on the day of his wedding and in which he was buried looked more and more like the one worn by the lower middle class in the city. At the open-air dances that brought a joyful end to the wheat or wine harvest, the violin and accordion replaced

the hurdy-gurdy. Girls and boys no longer danced with wooden shoes but with shoes made of leather. Instead of traditional folk songs and dances, they preferred polkas, waltzes, and mazurkas. The countryside no longer produced just enough food to feed the family. Its main aim was to grow crops to sell. Like the rest of the economy, agriculture was subjected to the law of the marketplace. If it produced too much, prices fell and ruined the farmers. This is why farmers formed their own unions, in order to petition the government to forbid the importation of foreign products.

A combine harvester in the Middle West. With the invention of the first harvester by McCormick in 1834, American farming became the most modern in the world. On the large grain farms in the Middle West, owners increasingly turned to companies offering to harvest their fields within a few hours. These harvesting teams arrived with an enormous machine, thirty horses, one driver, and three helpers.

Under the guard of armed soldiers, convicts board a ship for Guiana. Confined in cages, they traveled on a ship especially outfitted for their transport. They were only entitled to a daily one-hour walk on the deck.

Crime and Punishment

In Mongolia, nomads lived in villages of tents and did not have prisons. This crate was used instead.

Elegant stores, exhibitions, military parades, and reviews: the Belle Époque flaunted its luxury, wealth, and splendor. "Honest people," proud and happy, participated in this display and applauded the success of progress. Others, such as burglars, crooks, and swindlers, either chose to live outside the law or were forced to do so because of extreme poverty. Some, like anarchists, refused everything. They were opposed to the State, money, the army, ownership. They declared war on society and its leaders. Sovereigns and politicians were the targets of assassination attempts with revolvers, bombs, or knives.

Apprehending these enemies of order was the business of the police, who tracked them down with some of their best sleuths. They had modern and scientific means at their disposal. Keeping files on measurements enabled investigators to consult the record of any delinquent in the country. Each person arrested was described in the most minute detail. Height, the form of the face, nose and ears, color of eyes and hair, and distinguishing marks were all recorded. The face and profile of suspects were systematically photographed. Fingerprints could be compared but were not always taken.

Crime evolved with modernism. In the United States, train robberies replaced stagecoach attacks. The appearance of banks was immediately followed by holdups. The automobile was also used for criminal purposes at the beginning of the century. In 1911 the "tragic bandits" of the "Bonnot gang" terrorized the population of

Paris and its surrounding areas, eluding police attempts to arrest them. They used stolen cars to commit their crimes and did not hesitate to kill.

The law was harsh with thieves and criminals. The smallest theft meant several months in jail. In France, where murderers were judged by a people's jury, the jurors were chosen by drawing names out of a hat from lists mainly comprised of landowners and individuals living off private incomes. The lawbreaker who attempted to take other people's property was severely punished. A swindler or gangster was easily sentenced to twenty years of forced labor, but a cheated husband who killed his unfaithful wife could be acquitted on the grounds that it was no longer a murder but the redressing of a ridiculed honor!

Each city had its foreboding prison with gray sinister walls. Packed into tiny squalid cells, the prisoner lived under the custody of the prison governor and the guards. In Western Europe and the United States, depriving prisoners of food and placing them in solitary confinement replaced whipping, which was still in use in Russia and China to punish recalcitrants. But those who governed had long since stopped considering prisons a means of returning honest men, women, and children to society. Anyone who got out of prison was convinced theft and crime were the only roads to survival.

Penal colonies were a way of getting rid of "cases" whose rehabilitation seemed hopeless. France deported hardened criminals and notorious vagabonds to Guiana and New Caledonia. In Russia, the immense area of Siberia was put to good use by convicts whose families could go with them, without any hope of return. It was also the place where the Czar exiled all his political opponents.

Except for Portugal, Holland, and Norway, every country in the world applied the death sentence in 1914. The gallows, firing squad, sword, or guillotine were the terrible instruments of execution, an event that often took place in public, in the early morning hours, in front of the prison. Crowds always gathered to shudder at the most despicable of performances.

On December 9, 1893, the French anarchist August Vaillant threw a bomb into a filled Chamber of Deputies, slightly wounding a few deputies but not killing anyone. At the end of a speedy trial, Vaillant was sentenced to death. On February 5, 1894, in the early morning hours, the prison gate opened. Vaillant appeared. At the foot of the "wood of justice," Mr. Deibler, executioner, stood upright and solemn. His helpers grabbed hold of the sentenced man, who only had time to shout: "Down with bourgeois society, long live anarchy!" before kneeling under the blade of the guillotine.

Reading, Writing, and Arithmetic

"Our industrial prosperity depends on the rapid organization of elementary education. Providing technical training...to uneducated workers...is a waste of time. If we continue to leave our labor force without skills, it will be outclassed in world competition, despite its strong muscles and its determined energy..." The English Parliament made primary schooling mandatory in 1870. The decision was not made out of sympathy for the poor but out of an asserted sense of utility: "Education pays off!"

In France education was mainly the work of the Republic, which strived to take the teaching of children out of the hands of the clergy. In 1881 and 1882 Jules Ferry had laws passed aimed at providing all French citizens with "equal opportunities." Free and compulsory State education was created.

A school was built in each town, and its teacher was a graduate of a teachers' training school. This person had to try to teach a moral code acceptable to all parents, regardless of their religion. Being free, the school was open to all children, both rich and poor. Compulsory until the age of twelve, it had to teach all children to read, write, and count.

School was, above all, a way of uniting the French into one nation. Class subjects were the same in all the districts and even in France's colonies, where young Africans had to recite that their ancestors were Gauls! However, some differences were tolerated. In the small country school, for example, the teacher taught children of all ages in one classroom. In city schools, each age group had its own teacher. At the end of the pupils' studies, the same primary graduation certificate was awarded to all children.

In order to pass, the candidates had to take down a twenty-line dictation without making more than four mistakes, write a short essay that was also judged for its penmanship, solve arithmetic operations and two difficult problems, and answer history and geography questions. They had to know the fifty most important dates in the history of France, the names of all the districts and their major towns, and be able to locate France's colonies on the map. With all this knowledge, it was possible to become a good worker, an employee in a business, or a low-ranking government servant.

But children of wealthy parents very rarely went to the "town" school. They went to private schools, or lycées, where a tuition had to be paid and books and materials purchased. Their studies were longer and they learned Latin, Greek, and literature. They prepared for the baccalauréat, a diploma that enabled them to enter a university. In 1880, girls' lycées were created, but the number of pupils was still small.

For children of the lower classes, the only way to get into a lycée and obtain the baccalauréat was by passing an examination that entitled them to a grant for the remainder of their studies. But in 1900, not even 10 percent of French children in lycées were of working-class parents!

At the beginning of the twentieth century, in industrialized countries, most people

The newsstand and the pillar-shaped billboard, covered with posters announcing various forms of entertainment, were familiar to most Parisians during the Belle Époque. Almost everyone in Paris could read.

knew how to read. The printing press was in its golden age. With the invention of the Linotype, whole lines of type could be set quickly, using a keyboard rather than the hands. The rotary press made it possible to print and fold 100,000 newspapers per hour. These advances resulted in lower prices at the newsstands (one penny in London, two cents in New York, five centimes in Paris). With the telegraph and telephone, news arrived rapidly in the editing rooms of dailies. Transported by train and distributed nationwide, the large national dailies reached sales of from 500,000 to 1,000,000 copies. In order to attract a greater number of readers, newspapers published novels by popular writers of the time in serial form. Illustrated supplements with color prints and photos told the day's events, showed the latest inventions, dramatized accidents and natural catastrophes. Very soon, industrialists grasped the importance of the press. They paid a lot of money to place their "ads" in papers, and they financed sports events (especially auto races) organized by the newspapers.

But the press also played a primary role in forming public opinion. Most newspapers did not miss an opportunity to demonstrate their nationalism. In Germany, France, and Italy, some newspapers even went so far as to advocate war.

In her fine handwriting, the school teacher has written the date and moral maxim on the chalkboard. This was the first exercise of the day. A map is facing the table of measurements. The books in the library are placed in careful order on the bookshelves, located on both sides of the chalkboard. The pupils, in their black smocks, surround their teacher. The cross of honor hangs from the neck of the brightest student.

A world-famous spa in Vichy, France. Since the middle of the nineteenth century, spa towns were the gathering places for people more fashionable than really ill. Most spas specialized in digestive ailments and gout, the "rheumatism" of heavy eaters. For those who lived indulgently during the Belle Époque, the treatment was a brief moment of relative austerity.

Health Care

In 1900 medicine had become a science. Although doctors trained in schools of medicine were not able to cure all diseases, they no longer killed through ignorance. Bleedings were no longer administered except in exceptional cases. A century before, they were an essential part of any treatment.

Hospitals, built in large numbers by the State or charitable institutions, had up to one hundred persons in each of their large common wards. Through the work of biologists, the origin of diseases had become better known. Louis Pasteur had been the first to isolate and observe disease-causing bacteria, while the German bacteriologist Robert Koch had discovered the bacillus of tuberculosis. Surgeons now performed surgical procedures with anesthetics in the form of chloroform. They followed a very strict code of hygiene, whose absence in the mid 1800s caused the death of more than half of those who had surgery. They fell victim to infections.

But blood transfusions still remained risky. Blood types had still not been discovered. Donators were usually relatives of the sick persons, and the transfusion occurred directly from the vein of the donator to that of the receiver.

In cities and small country towns, the number of doctors and pharmacists increased. They had at their disposal medi-

This French poster advertises a new toothpaste. Brushing one's teeth was a new habit in 1900 and concerned only a very small percentage of the population. A visit to the dentist was rare. "Teeth pullers" still roamed the countryside. In families, it was not unusual to see a member's aching tooth pulled by tying it to a string, attaching the string to a doorknob, then slamming the door shut. Many old people had no teeth at all!

cines capable of calming pain and lowering fevers. Quinine had been in use since 1820, and aspirin appeared in 1906. However, the healing process was often very long. Influenza could keep a person bedridden for weeks if it did not kill him! Weakened by a fever that may have lasted for days, patients needed a long period of convalescence to recover their health.

At the turn of the century, the insane were locked up in sordid asylums because they were considered to be dangerous. Since 1880, however, numerous researchers had been interested in mental and nervous disorders. They believed the insane to be ill, just as a person suffering from a physical ailment is ill. In Paris, between 1880 and 1890, Professor Jean Charcot demonstrated that brain lesions were responsible for certain disturbances. He attempted to treat his patients through hypnosis.

In Vienna, Sigmund Freud, who had been Charcot's student in Paris, proposed an explanation for certain mental illnesses. His method of treatment was called "psychoanalysis." In his view, emotions and shocks, experienced by the patient during childhood, were the causes behind such illnesses. By talking with his "psychoanalysist," the patient discovered the unconscious reasons for his illness and could be cured. Very controversial at the time, Freud's theories were the subject of great interest on the part of the aristocracy and upper class in Vienna.

More than healing, medical practitioners wanted to prevent disease. It was a long time, however, before vaccinations were accepted. Despite the fame of Pasteur's work, people were still afraid to put it to the test. In France it was not until 1902 that vaccinations against smallpox became mandatory, despite their existence for the past one hundred years!

In order to avoid outbreaks of diseases in large cities, hygienic measures were taken, such as disinfecting schools and forbidding a child with a contagious disease from attending class.

Tuberculosis was the most dreaded disease of all. A vaccination had not yet been found and it was responsible for 20 percent of the deaths in Europe's cities. In order to fight it, doctors and governments mobilized all their energy. In Paris, in 1901, a league of "anti-spitters" distributed pamphlets, brochures, newspapers, and badges in order to

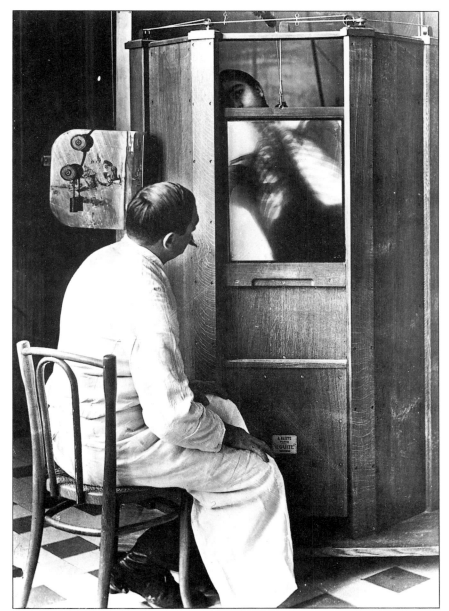

persuade the public not to spit on the ground! Doctors advised parents who could afford to do so to send fragile children to a sanatorium at the seaside or in the mountains for a few weeks. In 1900 doctors were able to detect on the lungs the first effects of the horrible disease. This was made possible by radioscopy, the examination of the internal structure of the body by means of X-rays, discovered in 1895 by the German physician Wilhelm Roentgen.

Although progress in the field of medicine had been enormous, still very few people went to see the doctor. Most people continued to care for themselves with "home remedies." Leeches were still placed on the body of a person suffering from indigestion! Glass cups were placed on the back of someone with a fever! At the slightest sign of a child's coughing, a vigilant mother would apply a mustard plaster.

Through radioscopy, the doctor is able to see through the body of his patient and examine his organs and bones. Harmless in small doses, X-rays cause burns and skin cancer to those exposed to them too often. The first doctors to use X-rays fell victims to this. It was not long before doctors learned to protect themselves by wearing heavy lead aprons.

The pilgrimage of Muslims to Mecca at the beginning of the century. Coming from all corners of the Islamic world, the pilgrims went seven times around the Kaaba, the holy city's sacred shrine.

Religions

In the face of the scientific progress made in one century, many scientists, philosophers, and writers believed religion would disappear. They were wrong. On the contrary, the beginning of the twentieth century witnessed a huge wave of religious fervor.

In Europe, Catholics comprised nearly half the population. Although the city-living middle class and workers no longer went to church regularly, they continued to marry there. Baptisms and especially their children's First Communion were more than ever before occasions for family reunions. The Church did much to retain its faithful worshipers. Every year, pilgrimages to Lourdes in France attracted the sick and their relatives in search of miraculous cures. In 1908 there were more than one million of them! Pope Leo XIII proclaimed in his encyclical *Rerum novarum* that Christian charity could not tolerate an employer who left his workers in a state of poverty. But his successor, Pius X, severely condemned Catholics who, on the pretext of modernizing religion, interpreted the Gospel in their own way and tried to come closer to Protestants and Orthodox worshipers.

The Orthodox Church was especially predominant in Russia, where the czar used the popes (Orthodox priests) to fight any attempt toward change. He also took advantage of the large number of Orthodox Christians in the Balkans to further Russia's interests.

Because of the emigration of the British and Germans to various parts of the world, Protestant churches could be found all over. These churches proliferated in the United States, and numerous Protestant missions were set up in Africa and Asia. In contrast to Catholics, who had to obey an authority considered as infallible as the Pope, Protestants adapted their religion more to the realities of the modern world. Some of them, however, opposed scientific progress, which they believed contradicted the teachings of the Bible. A good example was their opposition to Charles Darwin's ideas on the evolution of species, which denied that God created the earth, animals, and humans in six days. They were opposed to his theories being taught to their children!

Jews formed minorities in every country in Europe, North Africa, and the Near East. In Eastern Europe, large Jewish communities retained their traditions, language (Yiddish), and culture. However, they were victims of harrassment from the Christian populations, which formed a majority. In Russia the army sometimes organized "pogroms," which occasionally ended in massacres!

In Western Europe, Jews were less numerous and better integrated. They were victims of less violence but often the subject of virulent anti-Semitism. In order to defend themselves, a Hungarian Jewish writer, Theodor Herzl, proposed to Jews in 1896 that they emigrate to Palestine and create their own State. Zionism had been born. In 1914 only 150,000 Jews left their homelands for Palestine, but many others were to follow later.

In the rest of the world, Hinduism in India, Shintoism in Japan, and Buddhism in China experienced a rebirth of fervor in the face of Christianity,

In Mukden (Manchuria), the gate and brick tower of a Buddhist temple, photographed in 1912.

which Western missions attempted to impose. But it was Islam especially that made tremendous progress. In Africa new mosques were built. Boats and railroads made it possible for pilgrims to reach the holy places in and near Mecca more easily. From Morocco to Indonesia, millions of worshipers shared the same belief in Allah and Muhammad, his prophet.

At the end of the nineteenth century, a Persian, Jamâl Al Afghâni, proposed uniting all Muslims against Europeans. In the Middle East, Arab traders and princes dreamed of once again founding a large Islamic kingdom as powerful as that of the sultans in the Middle Ages.

A procession in Roscoff, a small seaport town in France. The girls wearing veils and crowned with white flowers are making their First Communion. They are carrying a shrine that contains a relic. Behind them, little girls with angel wings hold the ribbons of the banner of the Virgin Mary.

Nineteenth-century tastes in entertainment ran all the way from opera to Wild West shows. The great hall of the Paris Opera was often used for charitable gala performances and balls like the masked ball shown in the poster at the left. All Paris attended them. The poster at the right is an advertisement for Buffalo Bill's Wild West Show, which was as popular in Europe as it was in the United States.

Entertainment During the Belle Époque

The first cinema poster, published in 1896. L'Arroseur arrosé (A Practical Joke on the Gardener) was one of the first films by the Lumiére brothers. Here a respectable middle-class family and a "piou-piou," the nickname given to a young soldier in the French army, are enjoying the action.

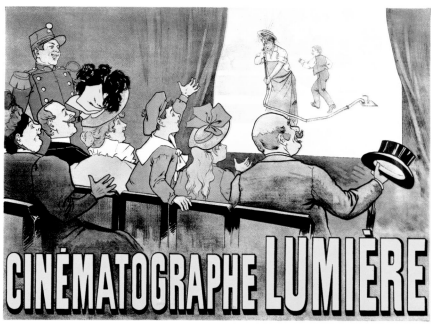

New York, London, Vienna, Berlin, and especially Paris were all capitals for shows, amusements and pleasure. The year 1900 was a noisy, flashy, vulgar, refined, artificial, and magical celebration.

For people who lived in the provinces, the wealthy businessman, the soldier on leave, or the foreigner just on a short stay, Paris was a place for meeting more people, experiencing more emotions and pleasures in a few days than one might experience in a lifetime. Entertainment could be found everywhere — on the street, at sidewalk cafés. For a few centimes, singers sold the music and words of popular tunes of the time whose refrains the public sang together. On the stage of a countless number of cafés, the French cancan had triumphed since the Second Empire. The dancers, dressed in satin and ostrich feathers, lined up in front of the audience and began to dance, lifting their legs and petticoats to the rhythm of the music. On the large esplanades, there were merry-go-rounds and Ferris wheels. At the race track on the boulevard de Clichy, one franc entitled a person to watch Roman chariot races, Gallic cavalry fights, or a stagecoach holdup.

Every evening nearly ten operettas or operas drew an audience wanting to be entertained or to hear the thrilling "bel canto" voices, whose admirers could be found in every class of society. Since 1890, opera had become more realistic. Situations and feelings the audience could experience were common themes.

In many of the great cities of the world during the Belle Époque, the theater was an especially popular form of entertainment. Audiences, made up mainly of the bourgeoisie, were moved by classical tragedies and such modern works as *L'Aiglon* and *Cyrano de Bergerac* by Edmond Rostand. The characters seemed to be straight out of history books. Audiences also enjoyed light theatrical entertainment, especially as it was performed in the theaters of the Paris boulevards. They laughed and applauded at the witty dialogue that often satirized the manners of contemporary society. To audiences living during the Belle Époque, such scenes were a refreshing departure from the family code of morals that had to be obeyed.

In Paris the cinematograph of the Lumière brothers opened its doors at the Grand Café on December 28, 1895. The films, which were still very short, were more an object of curiosity than a real show. However, in 1902, George Méliès made *Voyage to the Moon*, considered to be the first science-fiction film in history. It was a masterpiece. Max Linder made comic films that were extremely successful. Famous novels, such as *Les Misérables* and *Fantomas*, were brought to the screen. On the eve of the First World War, the cinema had become the "seventh art."

Tourism was also a pastime for the aristocracy and the well-off. Bathing at the seashore, which for a long time had been considered a way of taking care of one's health, drew a large number of fashionable people to palaces on the Normandy coast and French Riviera. The Alps were for bold walkers who took part in hikes organized by the Alpine Club or the Touring Club and which followed itineraries described in the Baedeker guide, the true Bible of the traveler during the Belle Époque.

A hike across a sea of ice above the French resort town of Chamonix. The women in the picture are wearing flower hats, corsets, waist petticoats, long dresses, high-heel boots, and carrying umbrellas. What a feat! Fashionable but not practical!

Transportation on the Land and in the Air

Since 1890, pedestrians and horses had been sharing the road with two new-comers — the bicycle and the automobile. The first invention consisted of a metal frame, two equal-sized wheels, and a chain drive. It was a convenient and inexpensive means of transportation that soon became popular. In France the army outfitted its liaison officers with them. And women rode them without fear of looking indecent.

The automobile, which in 1883 was equipped with a gas engine, remained a luxury item in Europe until 1914. Driving was considered to be more a sport than anything else. In the beginning, cars were rather slow but their speed rapidly increased. In 1899 the Belgian Jenatzy exceeded 62 mph in an electric car. Riding over cobblestone or dirt roads with wooden-rimmed wheels tired with iron was difficult and often hazardous. With the invention of rubber tires and especially the inflatable tire (developed by the Michelin brothers in 1891 and in use already in 1895 by Peugeot and Daimler), riding comfort greatly improved.

The first automobiles were produced on a unit basis by small manufacturers who supplied the customer with a chassis and engine "tailored to the person's needs" by a coachbuilder. In 1903 French workshops built 30,000 cars. This was over half the world's production. French engines manufactured by the Marquis de Dion were sold and copied all over the world.

It was in the United States, however, that inexpensive automobiles were first produced. In 1914 Henry Ford introduced the assembly-line technique for the manufacture of the Model T. This car, brought out in 1908, did more to popularize the automobile around the country than any other single model.

"Flying in a contraption heavier than air is math-e-mat-i-cal-ly impossible!" asserted learned scientists and renowned academicians. Yet, on December 17, 1903, in a field in Kitty Hawk, North Carolina, Wilbur and Orville Wright flew 11 feet above the ground in a funny-looking machine. It was an air-plane! A year later, they tried again. This time it was no longer a flea's jump but a flight of 2 miles that they made in September 1905. They stayed in the air a whole half hour.

In 1908, the first aeronautical exhibition opened in Paris. Wilbur Wright was the honored guest. Among the others present was Louis Blériot, manufacturer of planes already renowned on all French airfields. He accomplished an astounding feat. On July 25, 1909, on board a monoplane he built himself, he crossed the English Channel. A few days later, he participated in the "Semaine de Champagne," the first big air competition to bring together Europe's best pilots and all the manufacturers. A public of specialists, sport lovers, and amateurs had a passion for flying and no longer talked about anything but propellors, elevators, stabilizers, rudders, and the advantages of the monoplane and the biplane. The press covered every feat on the front pages. Aviation had become a serious matter — one in which governments and the military began to take a great interest. By World War I, the pioneers of flying had become "knights of the sky" and aviation was making rapid technical progress.

July 25, 1909. Blériot's monoplane is off to glory.

Montparnasse Station, November 9, 1895. One of the most unusual accidents in the history of railroads. It prompted a wise and prudent decision to be made to build solid buffers at the end of the tracks.

The Birth of Modern Art

The history of modern painting began with *Les Demoiselles d'Avignon*. With this painting, Pablo Picasso broke with the rules of traditional art. Astounded by this reconstruction of the human figure in diamond shapes, cubes, and triangles, the public named Picasso and his followers "cubists." When a cubist painted an object, he represented several sides "simultaneously." On the same face, he painted eyes seen from the front and a nose seen from the side. Cubists also tried to depict on the same canvas the various stages of a single movement by

In 1900 a gust of creativity blew over European artistic life. Together painters, poets, musicians, and architects created new forms of expression.

Pablo Picasso: Les Demoiselles d'Avignon *(1907).*

breaking the movement down into its component parts. Until then, a work of art had represented motionless subjects. Now, throughout Europe, painters were attempting to introduce movement and simultaneity into their works.

In France the painter Robert Delaunay chose to express movement with color, which he said "broke the forms." His experiments with swirling color planes, circular forms, and curving lines in brilliant colors led the French poet Guillaume Apollinaire to liken Delaunay's style to music.

In Italy "futurists," such as Gino Severini were carried away with noise, speed, and mechanical energy. To them, movement meant freedom. "A roaring car...is more beautiful than the Victory of Samothrace," the poet Marinetti proclaimed in *Manifesto of Futurism* (1909). Movement in the modern city was more beautiful to the futurist than a motionless work of art.

In 1901 a Russian painter living in Paris, Wassily Kandinsky, painted what is considered to be the first purely abstract work. This painting depended entirely on the emotional significance of colors and form without figurative suggestion. Kandinsky believed in nonobjective art based on the harmony of color and form.

At the turn of the century, painters were looking into the heart of a rapidly changing society. Modern art was created out of this exceptional revolution.

Wassily Kandinsky: Abstract Watercolor *(1910).*

Robert Delaunay: La Tour rouge *(1911).*

Gino Severini: Blue Dancer *(1912).*

Music was also revolutionized. In France, with La Mer *(The Sea) (1905) by Claude Debussy, the symphony became an orchestral poem. The Russian Igor Stravinski caused a scandal with* The Rite of Spring, *composed in 1913. The Austrian school, with Arnold Schoenberg, Alban Berg, and Anton von Webern, were among the avant-garde of modern music and replaced the traditional scale with a series of twelve atonal notes that were linked only by their sequence. Pierrot Lunair by Schoenberg (1912) was the archetype of this "dodecaphonic" music, which contemporaries said grated on their ears!*

61

War At Hand!

Since 1908, not a year had gone by without the threat of war. In Morocco, opposition between French and German interests nearly degenerated into a conflict. Russia and the Austro-Hungarian Empire both watched with an interested eye as the small nations in the Balkans quarreled over scraps of the Turkish Empire.

Most of Europe's governments believed a "good and short war" would settle all their problems once and for all. The French wanted to recover Alsace and Lorraine. Adults in the Belle Époque had been raised with the desire to take revenge on Germany after the humiliating defeat inflicted on France in 1870. In order to satisfy the generals who thought a vast offensive by French soldiers would sweep away the German troops within a few weeks, deputies passed a law that made three years' military service mandatory for all young people. How could Germany resist with Russia, France's ally since 1894, crushing it in the East under the "steamroller" weight of its enormous army?

Great Britain, worried about Germany's economic progress and fearing the development of its war navy, drew closer to France and signed the *Entente Cordiale*. Now allied with the world's major sea power, France could face war with greater confidence and less fear.

In Germany, the kaiser William II knew that France wanted revenge. However, to thwart its plans, he mobilized the best army in the world. Together with his allies, Austria-Hungary and Italy, the Reich formed a solid bloc in the center of Europe. But Italy did not want to sacrifice its soldiers for Germany's interests, and even less for those of the Austrians, who still ruled over regions where a majority of Italians demanded their annexation to Italy. German military officers persuaded the kaiser to act quickly. "Now there is still time; two years from now, it will be too late!" In 1913 Germany was ready. The next occasion for starting a war would be the right one.

On June 28, 1914, on a hot and sunny morning, the archduke Francis Ferdinand, nephew of the old emperor of Austria Francis Joseph and inheritor to the throne, was on a visit to Sarajevo, a town in Bosnia, one of the two Slav provinces in the south annexed by Austria-Hungary in 1908. Despite assassination threats, the archduke, accompanied by his wife, had decided to go on with the trip. Although the police had been alerted, very few were on duty. A bomb was thrown into the convertible car in which the archduke was riding. With a reflex of his hand, he pushed it away. It exploded a short distance away, wounding a few onlookers.

After the welcoming ceremony at the town hall, which took place in an atmosphere of extreme coldness, the princely couple stepped into their car. The photographer, who centered them in his viewfinder, was not at all aware that he was taking the last picture of the archduke alive! Two minutes later, at an intersection, the driver hesitated and slowed down. A young man pushed his way through the crowd, holding a revolver. He shot twice, killing the archduchess and the archduke Francis Ferdinand. Both collapsed, dead!

While the world was not immediately aware of the importance of this event, Austrian investigators soon showed that the young 19-year-old assassin belonged to a terrorist organization headed by Serbians who had sworn they would take back the Southern Slav provinces from Austria.

The Austrian government, backed by Germany, demanded that Serbia allow its inspectors to make investigations on Serbian territory. The king of Serbia refused. On July 18, Austria declared war on the country. Russia, in order to help the small country, mobilized its army. Now the tangle of alliances and secret treaties signed between the various European powers was set into motion. Germany mobilized against Russia and declared war on August 1. France mobilized in turn on the 2nd. On the 3rd it was at war with Germany, which had invaded the neutral country of Belgium in order to better surprise the French army. On August 5th, Great Britain joined in the war. Nothing or no one could now stop the terrible war machine. Eventually, the United States with its military and industrial might would be drawn into the European conflict.

In France and in Germany, the announcement of general mobilization caused scenes of jubilation. To the sound of military music, Europe rushed headlong, a flower in its gun, into the First World War.

Four Stars of 1900

politan Opera House. The "great Caruso" became a social phenomenon. He was the living myth of the Italian seducer — generous, funny, friendly. With the invention of the phonograph, Caruso's golden voice could be heard by a large public. He recorded everything, from famous opera songs to popular tunes of the time. His death on August 2, 1921, in Sorrento, Italy, deprived opera of a tenor considered by many to be the greatest of all time.

Caruso dressed as a cowboy in Puccini's The Girl of the Golden West. *(December 1910).*

Caruso, the Man with the Golden Voice

March 1900. A young Neapolitan tenor made his sensational debut at the Bolshoi Theater in Moscow. Before the czar and the court, Enrico Caruso sang Verdi's *Aïda.* Every evening, whether the tenor sang *Faust* or *Le Bal Masqué,* the enthusiastic audience stamped its feet and applauded, interrupting the performance and obliging him to do an encore of these great songs.

Caruso's career was now marked by successes. Milan, South America, Prague, Paris — he triumphed everywhere. In New York the audience of Italian immigrants went wild over his first appearance at the Metro-

Boni de Castellane, Dandy and Deputy!

The Chinese pedicurist had just put nail polish on the toenails of the Count de Castellane. The "beau Boni" (the nickname given him by the elite of Paris) put on his silk socks, a suit, and a cream-colored overcoat. He then placed a matching top hat on his head and picked out a gold-ringed ivory walking stick. He went to the stables, whose red velvet-lined stalls were lit by electricity. He stroked the head of his favorite thoroughbred, which he fed a brioche soaked in milk. Where did the incredible wealth of a noble descended from a family as authentic as it was penniless come from? America! In 1894 the Count went to visit the United States. There he met and married the orphan daughter of the late Jay Gould, king of the railroads! She was a very young lady "with a beautiful dowry," stated Boni, and an annual income of three million dollars. Returning to Paris, the Count de Castellane and his new wife moved into one of the most sumptuous mansions on l'avenue du Bois. To celebrate the Countess's twenty-first birthday, a party was given on the

lake in the bois de Boulogne. There were 250 guests and the event cost a total of 300,000 francs (a worker earned 5 francs a day). In 1898 the Count de Castellane was elected deputy of the Basses-Alpes from his "fief" of Castellane. He was a representative of the People!

The Great Sarah Bernhardt

"Sublime, divine"…there do not seem to be enough adjectives to describe the audience's enthusiasm as the curtain fell on the play's last line by Sarah Bernhardt. The great actress had been on the stage for almost forty years when the year 1900 made its entrance. Her age remained a secret discreetly kept by a group of faithful admirers. Famous for the purity of her voice and the grandiloquence and pomposity of her performance, Sarah Bernhardt tri-

umphed in performances the world over, from Canada to Australia, from Russia to Argentina. Her restless life, her extravagances, the incredible luxury with which she had her apartment decorated were all scoops for newspapers always on the lookout for news of the queen of the stage. In 1905 Sarah Bernhardt suffered an injury to her knee. This injury resulted in the amputation of her leg in 1915. But this did not stop her from acting. Sitting or lying down, she continued to perform until 1922, one year before her death.

Sarah Bernhardt in Edmond Rostand's L'Aiglon.

Verdi — Patriot and Composer

On January 27, 1901, the Italian composer Giuseppe Verdi passed away at the age of eighty-seven. Verdi's reputation as an outstanding composer and great patriot had been established when, in 1842, he wrote his opera *Nabucco*. The opera was based on a biblical theme and contained a chorus sung by a group of Jews held in captivity. This chorus was

adopted by the Italian public as the anthem of the movement to liberate Italy from Austrian domination and unite it into one nation. Between 1843 and 1845 Verdi composed six more operas which also expressed patriotic sentiments.

"Viva V.E.R.D.I.!" was scrawled by Italian patriots on walls throughout Milan. In this way they paid homage to the musician laureate of their movement and boldly announced

their desire to see Victor Emmanuel II (king of Sardinia) become king of a united and independent Italy (*Vittorio Emmanuele Re D'Italia*). When the Italian monarchy was proclaimed in 1861 Verdi was elected to the first parliament.

He continued to compose operas which were played with success throughout the world. Italians the world over hummed his great tunes. Honored at the end of his life as a patriarch, Verdi did not want a state funeral. Instead, his body was placed in a hearse usually used for the poor and taken to the cemetery in Milan. A silent crowd was his escort.

Glory to sports: Rugby was the fashionable sport among Parisian students during the Belle Époque. (Fresco by Guyonnet at the Lakanal de Sceau Lycée, 1899).

The Paris World's Fair and Olympic Games

In 1900 Parisians had still not forgotten the splendors of the 1889 World's Fair. Only now were they becoming accustomed to the Eiffel Tower, which had been built for this occasion. Nonetheless, the Third Republic was organizing a new fair to celebrate the new century. The 1900 World's Fair was to be the largest and most sumptuous fair ever organized. From the Trocadéro to the Champ-de-Mars, from the roundabout at the Champs-Elysées to the esplanade of the Invalides, and along the quais of the Seine River, Paris became a worksite. Wooden and stucco pavilions, Swiss chalets, Indian temples, and Chinese pagodas rose rapidly. All together they housed 83,000 exhibitioners and received nearly 50 million visitors! There was something for everyone. Those passionately interested in technical progress spent hours in the electricity pavilion, art lovers admired the collection of sculptures brought together under the glass roof of the Grand Palais, those with a bit of curiosity went to see "the moon from less than three feet away," thanks to the 197-foot telescope at the optical pavilion!

The fair was an imaginary trip to a foreign destination. The Swiss village depicted on cardboard a valley in the Alps with its castles and chalets. Even dairy cows were shown grazing! The around-the-world pavilion allowed its visitors to accomplish in one hour what Jules Verne's hero Phileas Fogg did in eighty days.

In order to enable visitors to see everything without tiring themselves out, an electric railroad, ancestor of the elevated railway, was built. There was even a moving sidewalk baptized "the street of the future."

In the avalanche of light, music, and fountains, an event went by almost unnoticed. It was the Olympic Games! On June 23, 1894, in the large auditorium of the Sorbonne University in Paris, the Olympic Games were officially reinstated. An Olympic committee was created, with Baron Pierre de Coubertin as its secretary. "Citius, Altius, Fortius!" (Faster, higher, stronger!) was the motto athletes the world over would make triumph every four years in the "renewed Olympic Games." The first *modern* games took place in Athens from April 5–10, 1896. The event was a great success and drew a crowd of more than 50,000 persons for the opening ceremony. But in 1900 the Olympic Games were entirely overshadowed by

proaching today's records: 10.83 feet for pole vaulting, 6.23 feet for the high jump, 11.5 seconds for the 100 meter flat race, 119.75 feet for the discus thrower. But the competitors were amateurs. Many were simply motivated by a sense of sportsmanship. Theato, for example, winner of the marathon in a little under three hours, was the gardener of the stadium in which the games were taking place! Since there was no swimming pool, the swimming events took place in the muddy water of the Seine. The competitions included contests that today no longer exist such as the 60 meter underwater swim, or the 200 meter swim with obstacles in which the swimmers had to climb over barrels in the middle of the race.

The 1900 Olympic Games were a victory for America. Of the 23 gold medals, 17 were won by the Americans.

The Electric Fairyland building and the fountains of the Château d'Eau during a nighttime celebration in Paris.

the World's Fair. The various competitions took place in the stands. Fencing was held at the cutlery stand! Only the athletic events were to be held in a stadium, in the park of Boulogne, where 600 athletes from twenty countries came to compete against one another. Their performances were far from ap-

Garin, winner of the first Tour de France in 1903.

The first Tour de France

On July 1, 1903, the chief editor of the French sports newspaper *Auto,* Henri Desgrange, announced to his readers the departure of the first cycle race, the Tour de France. There were six stopover points: Paris-Lyons, Lyons-Marseilles, Marseilles-Toulouse, Toulouse-Bordeaux, Bordeaux-Nantes and Nantes-Paris. The sixty competitors, with their caps and mustaches, carried with them all the tools necessary for repairing their bikes. Covered with dust, having ridden in temperatures above 86°F, the Savoyard Garin won the race. He covered 1,491 miles in 94 hours and 33 minutes. That meant an average riding speed of 16 mph.

The Olympic Games pole-vaulting competition took place at the Racing Club of France. The world record at the time was 10.83 feet with a rigid bamboo pole.

As 1900 Imagined the Year 2000

The arrival of the twentieth century encouraged journalists, film-makers, and illustrators to imagine what the year 2000 would be like. With an optimistic belief in unlimited technical progress, they headed in the direction indicated by Jules Verne. The top illustration depicts a twentieth-century tailor as a robot. The middle illustration shows the imagined ancestor of the modern school computer — a machine that eats books. Knowledge from the books enters the brains of the pupils through wires running directly from the machine to the pupils' heads. The bottom illustration shows the Paris sky, which has become a great boulevard, where conductors, riding on strange contraptions, ensure the steady flow of traffic. It appears that the illustrator was not able to imagine differences in dress, even though fashions change very quickly.

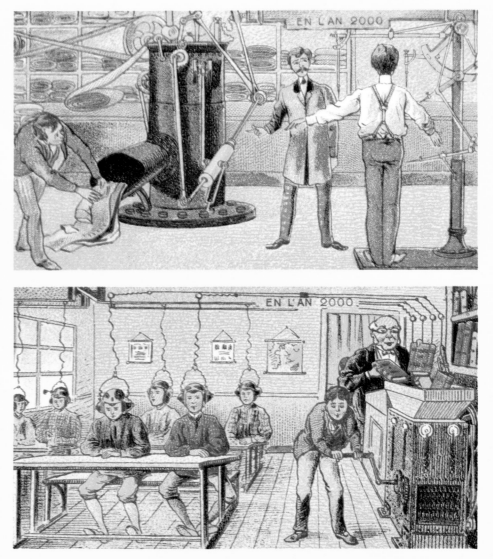

Glossary

Alliance A group of countries united in a common cause.
Anti-Semitism The persecution of, or discrimination against, members of the Jewish religion.
Archipelago A large group of islands.
Asylum An institution where the mentally ill are given care and shelter.
Autonomy A state or nation that is self-governing.

Belle Epoque The French term which refers to the "Gay Nineties".
Boxer Rebellion The uprising that took place in China from 1899–1900. It was meant to end foreign influence and drive foreigners from the country.

Capitalism An economic system in which land, factories, farms, and businesses are privately owned and operated.
Colony A territory that is far from the country that it is governed by.

Emigration The act of leaving one place or country and settling in another.
Empire A group of countries, territories, or peoples united under the rule of one government. An empire is ruled by an emperor (male) or an empress (female).

Famine A time when there is a severe shortage of food in one place.

Industrial Revolution The period of great economic and social change during the 18th and 19th centuries that was brought about by advances in agriculture and technology.

Missionary Someone who is sent to a foreign country by a church to spread and teach its religion.
Monopoly A situation in which one person or company has complete control over a product or service.
Mortality rate The death rate.

Obscurantism An opposition to the spread of knowledge, progress, or reform.

Penal colony An overseas settlement where criminals are sent for punishment.
Protectorate Treaty A treaty between two states in which the weaker state gives up the management of all of its more important international relations.

Reich The German word for "empire".

Socialism An economic system in which land, factories, farms and businesses are owned and operated by the government or the people as a whole.
Suffrage The right to vote.

Zionism A movement which at the turn of the century began to fight for the establishment of a homeland for Jews in Palestine. This eventually led to the establishment of the state of Israel in 1948.

Index

NORWAY

SWEDEN

FINLAND

Oslo

Stockholm

Helsinki

Mosc

NORTH SEA

BALTIC

SEA

DENMARK

RUSSIAN EMPIRE

GREAT BRITAIN
AND IRELAND

Copenhagen

NETHERLANDS

Berlin

London

The Hague

GERMAN

Brussels

BELGIUM

EMPIRE

L.

ATLANTIC OCEAN

Paris

Danube

Vienna

FRANCE

AUSTRIA-HUNGARY

Bern

SWITZERLAND

BLA

SEA

ROMANIA

Bucharest

Belgrade

ITALY

Sarajevo

BULGARIA

MONTENEGRO

SERBIA

Sofia

Lisbon

Madrid

Cetinje

Istanbul

PORTUGAL

Rome

ALBANIA

OTTOMAN

SPAIN

Vlorë

EMPIRE

GREECE

MEDITERRANEAN SEA

Athens

Europe in 1900

0   185 miles

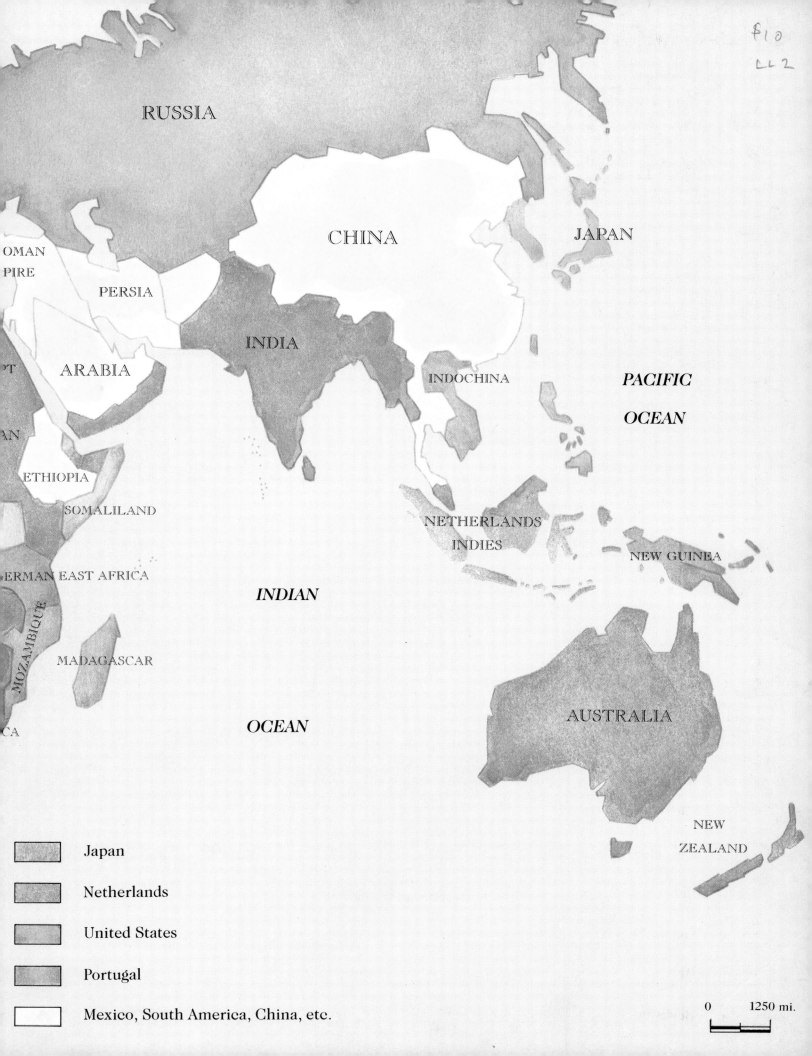

CONTENTS

Photographic Credits

ROGER-VIOLLET: p. 6–7 b; p. 10 b; p. 12 t; p. 13 t; p. 19 t; p. 28 b; p. 31 t; p. 33 t, b; p. 34 b; p. 38 t; p. 40 b; p. 42 t; p. 48 t; p. 50; p. 51; p. 52 t; p. 53; p. 54–55; p. 65 t; p. 67 bl; p. 69 / KEYSTONE: p. 8 b; p. 23 b / EDIMEDIA: p. 15 b; p. 17; p. 21 b; p. 26 t; p. 27 b; p. 30 b; p. 35 t; p. 36; p. 37 b; p. 40 t; p. 41 (Coll. G. Eastman, by Nickes Himes); p. 43 t, b; p. 45 b; p. 47 (Coll. G. Eastman); p. 49; p. 52 b; p. 57, 58, 59; p. 62; p. 68 (Album Robida) / LAUROS-GIRAUDON: p. 24 t (Dawant); p. 29 t; p. 38–39 (SPADEM); p. 56 b; p. 60 (SPADEM); p. 61 (ADAGP) / COLLECTION ALBERT KAHN, DÉPARTEMENT DES HAUTS-DE-SEINE: p. 14 b (by Stéphane Passet); p. 16 (by Stéphane Passet); p. 18–19 b (by Roger Dumas); p. 20 b (by Stéphane Passet); p. 22 b (by Miss Mespoulet); p. 32 t (by Stéphane Passet); p. 46 t (by Auguste Léon); p. 46 b (by Cuville); p. 48 b (by Stéphane Passet); p. 55 t (by Stéphane Passet) / COLLECTION J. L. CHARMET: p. 65 b; p. 66 t / COLL. PART. D. R. (by Casterman); p. 9 b; p. 32 b; p. 37 b; p. 54 t / COLLECTION JACQUES CUVINOT: p. 30 t; p. 31 b / COLLECTION J.C. CELHAY: p. 8 t; p. 11 t; p. 15 t; p. 21 t; p. 22 t; p. 23 t; p. 25 t; p. 25 b; p. 44 b / MUSÉE DE LA PUBLICITÉ, PARIS: p. 56 t; p. 67 t / ARCHIVES LAFFONT: p. 26 b; p. 44 ARCHIVES LAROUSSE: p. 64 / ARCHIVES DE L'ÉQUIPE: p. 67 br / PHOTOTHÈQUE R.A.T.P.: p. 45 t / SECRÉTARIAT D'ÉTAT AUX ANCIENS COMBATTANTS, D.S.I.H.: p. 63.
FRONT COVER: From the Musée de la Publicité, Paris. BACK COVER: Edimedia (coll. G. Eastman, by Nickes Himes).

Library of Congress Cataloging-in-Publication Data

Bosetti, Noël.
1900, the turn of the century.

(Events of yesteryear)
Translation of: 1900, la naissance du siècle.
Includes index.
Summary: Surveys events, people, and daily life around the world at the turn of the century.
1. History, Modern — 20th century — Juvenile literature. [1. History, Modern — 20th century] I. Sharp, Christopher. II. Title. III. Series: Jours de l'Histoire. English.
D422.B6713   1987   909.82   86-42663
ISBN 0-382-09296-1

Series directed by Noël Bosetti and Michel Pierre, professors of history, with the assistance of Elisabeth Sebaoun.

Project editor for the U.S. edition: Joanne Fink

© 1985 Casterman, originally published in French under the title *Les Jours de l'Histoire: 1900 La Naissance du Siècle.*

© 1987 English text, Silver Burdett Press. Published pursuant to an agreement with Casterman, Paris.

First published in the United States in 1987 by Silver Burdett Press, Morristown, New Jersey.

All Rights Reserved.